LEATHER FASHION DESIGN

646.11
STE

LAURENCE KING

Published in 2010 by
LAURENCE KING PUBLISHING LTD
361–373 City Road, London,
EC1V 1LR, United Kingdom
T +44 20 7841 6900
F +44 20 7841 6910
enquiries@laurenceking.com
www.laurenceking.com

TEXT © 2010 Francesca Sterlacci
This book was designed and produced
by Laurence King Publishing Ltd,
London.

A catalogue record for this book is available
from the British Library

ISBN: 978 1 85669 671 5

SENIOR EDITOR: Zoe Antoniou
COPY EDITOR: Fiona Biggs

DESIGN BY Melanie Mues,
Mues Design, London

Pages 2–3: Lost Art's Jordan Betten
created hand-painted, hand-laced bell
bottoms in plongé for his rock star
clientele in 2007.

Page 4: French designer Jean Claude
Jitrois created this orange jacket and
skirt in lambskin for his autumn/winter
collection in 2008.

SPECIAL THANKS TO: The Fashion
Group Foundation for supplying
many images from their archive in
this publication.
The Fashion Group Foundation, Inc.
8 West 40th Street, 7th Floor
New York, NY 10018, USA
T +1 212 302 5511
F +1 212 302 5533
www.fgi.org

Printed in China

The paper used for this book is from
sustainable forests.

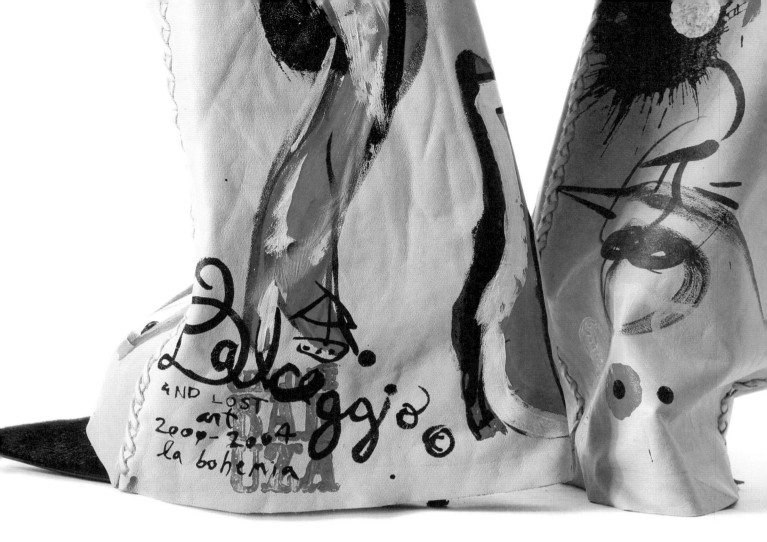

LEATHER FASHION DESIGN

FRANCESCA STERLACCI

LAURENCE KING PUBLISHING

CONTENTS:

FOREWORD 7
PREFACE 8

CHAPTER 1
LEATHER 11

INTRODUCTION 12
LEATHER AND THE FASHION INDUSTRY TODAY 12
LEATHER THROUGH THE AGES 14
THE TWENTIETH CENTURY 18
THE TWENTY-FIRST CENTURY 38

CHAPTER 2
THE TANNING PROCESS 59

WHAT TANNING DOES 60
THE MAJOR LEATHER MANUFACTURING STEPS 60
STORING SKINS FOR LATER USE 65
SORTING AND SELECTING SKINS 65
NEUTRALIZING 66
PREPARATIONS FOR DYEING 66
DYEING THE SKINS 66
STAKING 67
FINISHING TOUCHES 68
GRADING THE SKINS 69
SPRAY TREATMENTS 70
DECORATIVE TECHNIQUES 71

CHAPTER 3
THE DESIGN PROCESS 73

DESIGN INSPIRATION 74
ORGANIZING AND PLANNING YOUR COLLECTION 76
DESIGNING AND MERCHANDISING YOUR COLLECTION 78
THE REMAINING STEPS IN THE DESIGN PROCESS 78

CHAPTER 4
PLANNING 81

HAND 82
WEIGHT 82
SKIN SIZE 82
SKIN CHARACTERISTICS 84
PLANNING YOUR DESIGN 88

CHAPTER 5
CREATING A DESIGN/
SPEC SHEET 91
USING A DESIGN/SPEC SHEET 92

CHAPTER 6
SORTING, SHADING
AND CUTTING 103
SORTING AND SHADING 104
CUTTING 104
STORING SKINS 105
CUTTING TIPS 105

CHAPTER 7
PUTTING YOUR LEATHER
GARMENT TOGETHER 107
STITCHING 108
GLUING 109
PRESSING 109

CHAPTER 8
LININGS AND
REINFORCEMENTS 111
LININGS 112
UNDERLININGS 112
INTERLININGS AND FILLERS 112
INTERFACING 112
SEAM REINFORCEMENTS 113

CHAPTER 9
SEAM FINISHES 115
SEAM OPTIONS 116

CHAPTER 10
SEWING A SHIRT 119
CONSTRUCTING A SHIRT 120

CHAPTER 11
SEWING A PAIR
OF TROUSERS 127
CONSTRUCTING A PAIR OF TROUSERS 128

CHAPTER 12
SEWING A JACKET 139
CONSTRUCTING A JACKET 140

CHAPTER 13
LEATHER DEFECTS 161
BASICS 162
THE IMPORTANCE OF INDEPENDENT TESTING 162
HOW TO IDENTIFY AND SOLVE KEY QUALITY
CONTROL PROBLEMS 162

CHAPTER 14
FAUX LEATHER 169
FAUX SUEDE, FAUX GRAIN AND
FAUX PATENT LEATHER 170
CONSTRUCTION TECHNIQUES 174

RESOURCES 181
TIPS FOR PROPER LEATHER
GARMENT CARE 182
DIRECTORY 183
GLOSSARY 186
FURTHER READING 188
INDEX 189
CREDITS AND ACKNOWLEDGEMENTS 192

Related study material is available
on the Laurence King website at
www.laurenceking.com

FOREWORD

Security, sustenance and shelter from the elements are the most basic needs that must be satisfied for human survival, and over thousands of years we have demonstrated the intelligence required to satisfy those needs in far more sophisticated ways than any other species on the planet. The use of animal hides for clothing and shelter, developed as a by-product of the food supply by early man, was a key element in providing protection from the elements. Thousands of years have passed, and many other products, some natural, some man-made, have been adopted for use in the manufacture of clothing, but in all this time one still remains; leather. Over the millennia all that has changed is the tanning process and the tremendous variety of hides available.

As we moved from caves and other primitive forms of shelter, we also moved from fur-covered hides to skins that were tanned, cut, shaped and sewn to make clothing. As we became more sophisticated, other needs surfaced. There was a tension between the need to conform and the need to be different, pulling us one way and then another, and this led to the use of clothing as a tool to look the same, or to look just a little different, or to look very different. This is where the seeds of fashion are; the basis for differentiating ourselves from how others look, or joining in to look the same as others. Perhaps at one time a woolly mammoth cape was a status symbol; today it's a Prada bag or Gucci loafers.

Through the ages, leather has had an allure and a cachet. The words 'genuine leather' evoke quality, and, together with fine workmanship and beautifully tanned skins, this makes a leather-bound book, a leather handbag, briefcase or article of clothing, very, very desirable.

Leather Fashion Design is the most complete textbook available on the subject, providing a thorough, comprehensive overview of the history and uses of tanned leather throughout the ages. The outline of the tanning process is extremely detailed, yet easily understood. This 'how-to' guide will be utilized by students and industry professionals for years to come.

Jeanette Nostra (President) and Carl Katz (Director), GIII Apparel Group

Opposite: Lost Art designer Jordan Betten creates one-of-a-kind leather pieces – his desk is a treasure trove of inspiration.

PREFACE

My goal in writing this book was to create a truly comprehensive guide to leather and faux leather clothing design. The target audience is professionals currently involved in the fashion industry as well as students, teachers and home sewers who possess basic sewing skills, or anyone interested in working with leather.

Whether the reader is interested in the beginnings and historical evolution of leather and faux leather clothing, leather and faux leather design and construction, the leather tanning process or even the care and cleaning of leather, this book serves as an industry standard.

I wrote this book because so many of my students at the Fashion Institute of Technology in New York and other schools expressed a keen interest in learning more about leather apparel design. I was genuinely surprised to discover that no one had ever written a book on this subject specifically to educate both the serious design student or the professional already working in the leather apparel industry.

The world's first leather apparel design programme started at the Fashion Institute of Technology in 1997. *Leather Fashion Design* is intended for use not only in this programme, but also in fashion schools around the world. I hope that more design schools will feel that the book is the tool they need to create their first leather programme.

Leather Fashion Design is also a resource for hundreds of leather apparel manufacturers, who can use the book to help train their new employees in the jargon, techniques and good judgement needed to create, care for and sell leather garments. It contains an exhaustive historical section with many inspirational colour images from prehistoric times up to the present day. It illustrates, through a series of photographs and text, the changing face of leather garment design through the ages. In addition, the reader will become familiar with the designers who were, and are, influential in the industry.

The book explains the leather tanning process in layman's terms, and it also introduces the reader to the terminology used regularly by professionals in the leather apparel industry. It describes the various types of leather skins that are available for purchase around the world, providing a definitive index of the characteristics, size and end use of every type of skin, including exotic skins, such as fish and hippopotamus. Students will probably be surprised at the vast array of available skins. By knowing about these, the reader will be better equipped to choose the appropriate one for a particular design. The book also discusses the appropriate choice and handling of skins in detail.

The reader will learn all about the design process — the research, creative and merchandising planning process that can inspire a designer to create a successful line. The book instructs the reader on how to organize and plan a collection, explaining the process of designing, editing and merchandising a line, as well as describing how best to present it to clients, colleagues or employers, using theme/mood and style boards. In fact, the book provides examples of an actual themes and style board used by a major leather manufacturer.

There is also an explanation of how to complete and use a design/spec sheet. Here again, there is a compilation of design/spec sheets used by actual manufacturers.

Furthermore, there are instructions in the techniques involved in constructing leather garments, focusing on the way it is commonly done in the leather apparel industry. In fact, all the step-by-step instructions for constructing leather garments were photographed in an actual leather garment factory and later illustrated for clarity. The book's step-by-step sewing guide demonstrates the construction of three different garments: a shirt, a pair of trousers and a jacket. Armed with the techniques used to create these garments, you will be able to construct just about any leather garment.

You will also learn about the use of faux leather and suede, a discussion illustrated by a series of photographs beginning with Ultrasuede in 1971 to present-day faux leathers. How to cut, sew and handle this increasingly popular material is also covered.

Frank H. Rutland, former Techncial Director of the Leather Industries Research Laboratory, has contributed most of the insights on leather testing in the leather defects section. This chapter thoroughly describes many of the most common of these problems, suggesting practical ways to solve them.

The care and cleaning of leather skins and garments is also covered, and a list of recommended leather care products is included.

Finally, the book includes information on fabric apparel industry events, a list of leather publications, organizations and schools within a helpful resource directory.

Francesca Sterlacci

CHAPTER 1
LEATHER

Leather has a rich history. Ever since man discovered how to work with leather and harness its unique protective properties, it has been one mainstay of our wardrobe. In this chapter we will explore the uses of leather in clothing and in fashion, from its early origins to the high-fashion catwalk creations of today.

INTRODUCTION

Leather is a word that is synonymous with luxury, fantasy, fetish, beauty and sensuality. From the dawn of time to the present day, leather has evoked a passion within us that is unique. Whether it is its innate beauty, interesting grain, luxurious feel or intoxicating aroma, we are somehow mysteriously drawn to it. It conjures up a plethora of sensations in the brain, an inexplicable type of primal instinct.

From crude body coverings to the high-fashion world of haute couture, leather making has long been considered an art form. It has also been surrounded by contradiction and controversy. In some cultures leather making is a symbol of life, resurrection and even fertility, while in others it is considered impure and unclean. Some designers choose leather for its status, subtlety and durability, while others choose to boycott it, preferring artificial leather instead. Although most of us wear leather on our feet, not everyone can afford to wear it on their backs, thus securing its place in the world of luxury and privilege.

Despite a fascination with leather, most people are completely unaware of how it is made. However, whether chrome tanned, vegetable tanned or made in the next-generation organically certified tannery, it is a remarkable material that is worth studying. Though we live in the age of technology, the process of tanning and constructing a leather garment still, as in ancient times, involves a substantial amount of hands-on skill. The intricacies of **tanning** and the special skills involved in the design and construction of leather apparel can give the impression that leather should cost more than it does. The process is complex and time consuming, with each skin handled by at least 25 people before it reaches the consumer. No other material in the history of fashion can compare.

Leather is symbolic. It represents rebellion, as demonstrated in the 1950s' motorcycle jacket worn by movie star Marlon Brando in *The Wild One*, and later studded and chained by punk rockers in the 1980s and 1990s. Skin-tight leather jeans, first worn in the late 1960s and 1970s by rock legends Elvis Presley, Jim Morrison and Mick Jagger, are updated today in the form of sexy, stretch leather. Fringed **suede** jackets, once the uniform of cowboys and Native Americans, became the emblem of anti-establishment hippies during the 1960s. The use of leather in the aviator and bomber jackets worn during World Wars I and II symbolized the rough-and-ready soldier and hero. On the other hand, the black leather coat worn by the Nazi SS was a symbol of power that induced fear.

Leather is spiritual. Greek high priests slept in a **hide** to encourage prophetic dreams. Ancient Egyptians were buried with leather to protect them from demons. Young Native American girls still wear 'coming-of-age' dresses made of deerskin to celebrate their womanhood, and in Algeria a birth ritual called the Feast of the Lamb involves wrapping a newborn baby in a newly slaughtered lamb skin as part of a welcoming ceremony.

Leather protects. From the first crude body coverings to more sophisticated breastplates and chain mail, leather has provided protection from both the elements and the enemy. Whether used for chaparajos by American cowboys, Spanish *charros* and Hell's Angel bikers, or as bomber jackets worn by war pilots, leather is durable, functional and breathable, as comfortable in a rodeo as it is on a catwalk.

Leather is sexual. Jean Paul Gaultier's leather corset for Madonna and Thierry Mugler's infamous leather neck corset offered an empowering figure of female sexuality. Similarly, leather as a fetish material and as a symbol of power and submission was evidenced in the second skin catsuit worn by the heroine in *The Matrix* and in the dominatrix outfit worn in *The Story of O*. Designers Claude Montana, Gianni Versace and Azzedine Alaïa have used leather to define and accentuate the female form by designing body-sculpting skirts and bondage-style jackets and trousers.

No other material has as much versatility as leather and although it tries hard, PETA (People for the Ethical Treatment of Animals) just can't seem to knock leather from its throne. It will always hold a place in the fashion industry, just as it has had a place in history since the birth of humankind.

LEATHER AND THE FASHION INDUSTRY TODAY

Today, the leather industry comprises £30 ($50) billion of the £200 ($320) billion global fashion industry. Leather apparel is manufactured all over the world with the *best* leather garments made in Italy and the *most* leather garments made in China. Leather apparel is manufactured for all levels of the market, from the designer to the budget category.

Many of the top design houses, including Ralph Lauren, Calvin Klein, Versace, Donna Karan, Gucci, Chanel and Christian Dior routinely include leather in their collections. And, although the leather cycle is said to peak every three years, leather clothing can be found in stores all year round. No matter what the price point, leather attracts consumers like no other material can.

Inexpensive skins allow the average person the opportunity to own a leather garment, although better quality leather is still the

Previous spread: Gianni Versace's leather-studded bustier from 1992 is a stunning exposition of the sculptural possibilities of leather.

true mark of luxury. Price points for leather apparel can range from a pair of trousers in pig split at £35 ($60) to one in **plongé** at £1,200 ($2,000). Interestingly, the designer-brand customer who would ordinarily forego a style that has 'trickled down' to the budget market, seems not to mind when it comes to leather. Leather somehow transcends the fashion caste system.

In the first decade of the twenty-first century, the once logo-crazed consumer of the 1980s and 1990s began to move away from over-marketed clothing. A celebrity-endorsed product or a designer logo slapped on an item no longer guaranteed a sale. Consumers became savvier when making choices and products needed to stand on their own regardless of the brand name. Designers and manufacturers, now more than ever, are focusing on quality and design. They know that today's educated consumer can tell the difference between inferior quality and very good materials and workmanship. Leather's reputation as a high quality material is a major reason why so many designers choose to work in the medium, even if they have never included leather in their collection before.

At the same time, leather tanneries are experimenting with different processes and finishes, making leather even more desirable and unique. Special treatments such as laser cutting, embroidery and burnishing add a decorative touch, while the metallicizing of skins has been updated with ombré effects and pattern stamping. At the other end of the decorative scale, leather can now be washed and buffed to create a soft, rugged texture. Leather garments have also become more user- and wearer-friendly with the introduction of leather that can be machine washed and dried, and a special backing that enables leather garments to stretch while retaining their shape.

Where leather tanneries once strove to apply effects that made leather look more like fabric, the trend is now to make leather look more authentic, especially through the use of old-fashioned vegetable-tanning techniques. Although the more recent introduction of chrome tanning means that leather produced by the application of chemicals costs half as much as vegetable-tanned leather, the exquisite hand and feel of vegetable-tanned leather add to its exclusivity. Vegetable-tanned skins are tighter, less stretchy and more durable, and have an earthy smell as a result of the use of natural tannin extracts from trees such as the mimosa, quebracho and tara.

In these eco-conscious times, some designers, such as Stella McCartney, boycott leather altogether, while other designers favour vegetable-tanned leather instead of chrome-tanned. The result of this changing consciousness is that even the process of chrome tanning is becoming more eco-friendly, with advances in the environmental acceptability of chemical dyes and the disposal of tanning waste products.

In 1995, French designer Jean Claude Jitrois developed stretch leather in conjunction with DuPont de Nemours, and they have since continued to push the boundaries of the physical properties of leather.

LEATHER THROUGH THE AGES

We don't know which of our ancestors discovered the process of tanning leather – the science of preserving and softening animal skins – but alongside the preservation of food it was arguably one of the most important inventions in human history.

Our ancestors learnt how to preserve food by salting, smoking and drying, but none of these processes would render an animal skin suitable for comfortable clothing. Touching a dried animal skin is like touching a board. It was probably after much trial and error, and by accident, that someone created the first truly tanned, preserved skin, by drying it, boiling it with tree bark and then rubbing it with fresh animal fat, bending and working it until it became completely soft. This early tanner may also have discovered that since water and fat don't mix, the soft, slightly greasy skin was also waterproof.

The need to make warm clothing probably developed first in the colder climes of northern Europe. It is believed that Neanderthal man draped animal skins over his shoulders and may have used crude ropes to tie the skins around his waist or head, as evidenced in cave paintings. Based on a new DNA genetic study of the evolution of body lice, it is believed that humans began wearing clothing some 42,000–72,000 years ago, since body lice exist only when body coverings are worn. It is thought that these coverings were most probably made from animal skins.

Cro-Magnon man, who moved into Europe some 40,000 years ago, probably wore more sophisticated garments, laced or sewn together with string made from animal hides, using the bone needles found in archaeological sites. We even have evidence that man became preoccupied with fashionable clothing as early as 20,000–26,000 years ago. Skeletons excavated near Moscow in northern Russia were covered in thousands of mammoth-ivory beads arranged in patterns, indicating that these were hand-sewn on to a now-decomposed garment, presumably made of leather. The earliest surviving leather garment, a loincloth, however, dates back only to 3300 BC and was worn by Ötzi the Ice Man, discovered in a glacier in the Italian Alps in 1991.

Because our early ancestors could not write, and because the ravages of time have destroyed much of what our ancestors wore, we have to rely upon the earliest written and artistic records to trace leather's contribution to fashion history.

THE MIDDLE EAST

In Mesopotamia, somewhere between the fifth and third millennium BC, for example, the Sumerians used animal skins to create women's dresses. We know this from their depiction on urns and other vessels and in wall paintings. The use of colour suggests that they used organic dyes in the tanning process. We also know that the Egyptians were particularly adept at leather making. It is believed that they were highly skilled in mineral-, vegetable- and oil-based tanning methods. Leather artefacts have been found in tombs built as early as 3000 BC. From these, we know that the Pharaohs wore leather sandals. We also know that

Wall paintings provide us with some of our earliest images of leather tanning. Scenes depicting Egyptian craftsmen at work making leather shoes adorn the ancient tomb of Rekhmere, near Luxor-Thebes, from the Eighteenth Dynasty, New Kingdom.

they wore other garments made from leather. A loincloth of gazelle skin, worn by a workman in Ancient Egypt from the Eighteenth Dynasty, 1580–1350 BC, is almost perfectly preserved. It is on display at the Museum of Fine Arts, Boston.

The Old Testament makes numerous references to leather, crediting the Hebrews with the oak bark tanning process. Leather items were traded throughout the Mediterranean by the Phoenicians of Babylon, who were great seafarers. A red dye that they used is still known today as Phoenician Red.

THE FAR EAST

The ancient Chinese worked in leather to create elaborately decorated boxes, screens and chests. Their earliest method of tanning included a smoke and salt process, which was later replaced by a system that used animal fat, bone marrow and animal brains.

EUROPE

In 1873 a tannery was uncovered in the ruins of Pompeii in southern Italy, providing evidence that the Romans were making leather footwear, clothing and ornaments. The Etruscans, who lived between 750 and 500 BC, handed down their leather-working skills to the Romans, who went on to develop the craft, eventually setting up a tanner's guild. Initially, soldiers used leather for shields, breastplates and sandals, but while they were fighting the nomadic Teutonic tribes in the cold of northern Europe, they discovered that these tribes wore whole garments made of leather. They adopted the practice and returned to Rome wearing leather trousers called *braccae*.

As people became more skilled in the process of tanning, the range of artefacts and clothing manufactured from leather grew. In Spain, during the eighth century, the ruling Moors created a tanning process that produced the famous Cordovan leather, also called Spanish leather. This softly tanned goatskin is dyed in numerous colours and is often perfumed. It was popular throughout Europe and, by the fifteenth century, many homes contained wall hangings, upholstery, book covers, waistcoats and jackets made of finely detailed Spanish leather. Some of these objects were hand painted, carved, inlaid or stamped in silver or gold.

There are many examples across Europe of tanneries growing up beside other industries. Solofra, in Italy, is well known today for its many excellent tanneries. However, the town was originally famous for making gold leaf, used in the 1400s to decorate Italian buildings and their contents.

To make gold leaf, artisans pounded large ingots of gold into extremely thin sheets, using large hammers over a heavy leather pad. Because the pads took such a pounding over the course of a year, the artisans had to replace them quite frequently. Initially they had to import the leather at great expense, but eventually they started to tan their own leather to make the pounding pads. Many of them created sideline businesses selling leather saddles, whips and boots.

When the architectural sensibilities of Italy and Europe moved away from the frequent use of gold leaf, the families of craftsmen whose livelihoods depended upon gold leaf had to find another business to support themselves and many of them turned to tanning full time. Today, no one makes gold leaf in Solofra but it is home to more than 200 tanners.

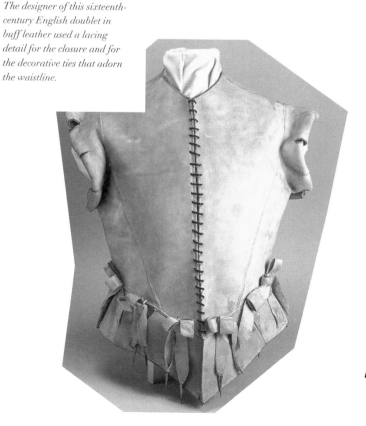

The designer of this sixteenth-century English doublet in buff leather used a lacing detail for the closure and for the decorative ties that adorn the waistline.

This seventeenth-century buff leather jerkin has whalebone stiffening in the collar and silver-gilt braid as a sleeve detail and on the front closure.

France offers another example of the tanning industry allying itself with another craft. In the seventeenth century the French nobility wore leather gauntlets and gloves. However, the tanning process left a disagreeable odour on the gloves, so the French bathed them in perfume. Since the tanneries were all in the south of France, perfume manufacturers would travel there to sell their products, eventually setting up their industry there permanently. Although the tanneries have long since moved, the perfume industry is still concentrated in Grasse, in the south of France.

As well as being fashioned into gauntlets and gloves, leather came to be used in fashionable clothing across Europe; in sixteenth- and seventeenth-century England it was used as it had been in ancient Rome, in the manufacture of protective clothing to be worn when working or fighting.

SOUTH AMERICA

While Europe advanced in the art of leather tanning and design, the Aztec, Mayan and Incan civilizations also advanced in their use of leather. They wore clothing made from the skins of indigenous animals, for example buck, buffalo and deer.

NORTH AMERICA

When the first settlers came to the New World, they brought their own methods of tanning. They were able to enhance these with the advanced tanning skills of the Native North Americans, including the technique of **oil tanning**. The Native Americans made teepees out of leather and decorated their leather clothes and moccasins with beads, feathers, porcupine quills and bones. Sometimes they painted scenes of famous battles on their leather.

By the late seventeenth century tanneries had appeared throughout the early American colonies. Borrowing from the Native Americans, the early settlers of the American West wore fringed buckskin jackets, waistcoats, chaps, boots and gauntlets. Sometimes their hats were made of leather or were leather trimmed.

EUROPE AND AMERICA IN THE NINETEENTH CENTURY

During the Industrial Revolution of the nineteenth century, American chemist Augustus Schultz invented a newer and faster method of tanning using chromium salts. Instead of taking weeks or months to tan a skin, this new method required only a few hours. In both America and Europe, engineers invented special machines to increase tanning productivity. In 1809, a leather splitting machine was patented, which could split leather to any desired thickness.

This Southern Cheyenne or Southern Arapaho girl's deerskin dress shows the sophistication of Native American tanning knowledge. It is decorated with glass beads, cowrie shells, cotton cloth and sinew thread. What makes it extra special is that it is cream-coloured, a particularly difficult colour to produce in a tanned garment.

When a young woman reaches puberty, the Mescalero Apache celebrate creation and their reverence for women during a four-day coming-of-age ceremony. This coming-of-age poncho and skirt from the early 1900s are made of buckskin, with heavily beaded fringing and beaded embroidery.

During the Indian Wars, the Apache served the US Army as scouts from 1871–1923. Since they were never issued uniforms, they created their own, as shown here in this shirt from the late 1800s. Made out of deerskin in the sacred pigment, yellow ochre, the shirts were ornamented with rows of buttons, fringing and beadwork.

American pioneer woman Calamity Jane (c. 1852–1903) wears a fringed leather jacket and leather trousers.

The corset, or stays as they were originally known, grew out of the stiffened bodice of fifteenth-century women's gowns. The familiar shape we recognize today is from the 1820s. Corsets were made from a variety of materials, including leather, that would provide a firm foundation. Here, yellow leather and whalebone are used to reinforce this English red cotton corset of 1883.

THE TWENTIETH CENTURY

1900–1930s

In the early 1900s, with the advent of the open automobile, wealthy motorists wore long leather motoring coats to protect them from weather and dirt. They also wore leather trench coats fashioned after the British military officer's coat. Leather and suede were also used in men's sports clothing. Leather entered the purely fashionable, rather than the functional, in the 1930s, when leather and suede became favourites with designers and head-to-toe looks appeared.

Designed to offer protection to those indulging in exercise, this golfing jacket dates from 1928.

The British film actress and director, Ida Lupino, wears a suede hat, shirt and skirt of the kind of outfit that became popular in the 1930s.

In the mid 1920s, Schott Bros. were the first manufacturers to put a zip on a jacket, revolutionizing outdoor wear. The Perfecto motorcycle jacket, named after designer and manufacturer Irving Schott's favourite cigar, made its appearance in 1928 and was popularized in the 1940s. This is the 'One Star' version, so-called because of the single star on each shoulder.

US fighter pilots of the 1940s were fully protected against the elements by their leather aviator jackets and trousers.

1940–1950s

The 1940s and 1950s saw two major developments in leather fashion. The first was in colour. Up until the early 1940s shades of tan, black, rust and brown predominated leather used for both menswear and womenswear. However, advances in the tanning process resulted in the availability of brighter colours, such as red, green and yellow, and designers began to take full advantage of the opportunities offered by producing multi-coloured garments. In the late 1950s and early 1960s, designers continued to experiment with the new leather colours. Bonnie Cashin was the first American designer to design extensively in leather and suede – her use of colours such as hot pink, red and mustard transformed the leather industry.

The 1940s and 1950s were also the era of the leather 'biker' jacket. Although the black leather biker jacket, the Perfecto, was first introduced in 1928 by the American company, Schott Bros., it didn't achieve popularity until the late 1940s when it became a symbol of rebellion and freedom. Originally made of horsehide and popularized in *The Wild One* (1953), starring Marlon Brando, it continues to be a 'fashion rebel' icon. Throughout the years it has been featured in films such as *Rebel Without a Cause* (1955), with James Dean, and in *Easy Rider* (1969). After the death of James Dean, who was wearing a Perfecto jacket when his car crashed in 1955, schools banned the jackets for many years. Over the years the black leather biker jacket has been associated with the late 1960s and early 1970s hard rock scene, punk rock, and it is the adopted 'uniform' of the motorcycle gang, the Hell's Angels.

Another popular jacket style of the 1940s was the flight or aviator jacket inspired by the Perfecto and manufactured for the US Air Corps. Even diehard army commanders, including General Patton, wore them during World War II. The look of an aviator jacket is still quite distinctive today, and it continues to create a unique image for the wearer.

Bonnie Cashin was Coach's first designer. The turn-key closure, seen here on this trio of colourful leather pieces, became her trademark.

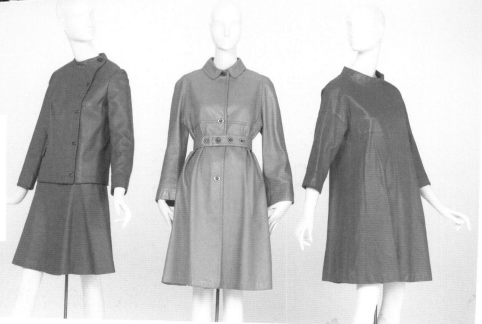

1960s

In 1960, leather design came into its own, enjoying tremendous worldwide popularity. While Bonnie Cashin continued to be at the vanguard of leather design in the United States with her combination ensembles of leather with fabric and knit, European designers, such as Nina Ricci, Manuel Pertegaz, Rudi Gernreich and Yves Saint Laurent took leather to the level of couture. Meanwhile, an abundance of leather clothing flooded the market, due in part to the hippie movement. Small boutiques, featuring handmade leather clothing and accessories that were fringed, beaded, braided, hand-laced and painted, prospered.

In 1964, Nina Ricci designed this floor-length leather evening coat. The very simple shape is complemented by the use of striking gold embroidery.

Viennese designer Rudi Gernreich was well known for working in alternative materials and creating far-out fashion. In 1966, he took to the jungle with his fun stencilled, hair-on calfskin suit.

Since much of the highest quality leather was produced in Spain, it was only natural that Spanish designers used leather in their collections. Barcelona's Manuel Pertegaz had a modern approach to fashion and in 1968 created a pair of brown leather chaps attached to a belt.

In 1967, Yves Saint Laurent created his Africa collection and, in 1968, introduced the safari suit into high fashion. This is the 1967 forerunner of the look, created in sleek, polished black leather.

1970s

Throughout the twentieth century, fashion trends trickled upwards as often as they trickled down from the heights of couture, and the 1970s were no exception. While some designers borrowed from the hippie trends of the late 1960s, others realized that adding leather garments to their collections would attract a more sophisticated customer. In doing so they repositioned black leather from 'rebel status' to fashion 'must have' in every woman and man's wardrobe.

Anne Klein's high-waisted black leather skirt of 1970 offered a perfect interpretation of current fashion trends and helped to upgrade Klein's image at the time.

Patchwork, very popular in the late 1960s, used leather scraps to create the look that was quite popular with the hippie crowd. By the 1970s designers such as Adolfo interpreted the look for the high-end market, taking advantage of the different colours with which leather could now be tanned.

As leather was fast becoming associated with slick, modern style, some designers, such as Giorgio di Sant'Angelo, went in a different direction, creating casual looks that included this 1978 embroidered suede Pocahontas dress, inspired by Native American costume.

1980s

In the 1980s designers created luxury clothing in leather and suede that consumed vast amounts of skin, using it as if it were fabric. Skin size was no longer a limitation – larger pig- and cowskins became increasingly popular as tanneries around the world began to copy the rich, luxurious hand of the finest European tanned lamb leathers and suedes.

French, English and Italian designers led the way, designing and inventing some of the most creative and saleable leather clothing. Giorgio Armani, Claude Montana, Azzedine Alaïa, Emanuel Ungaro, Valentino, Anne Marie Beretta and Vivienne Westwood were at the vanguard. There seemed to be no limitations. Anything that could be done in cloth could be done in leather. The various weights and choices of skins developed by tanneries, and the vast assortment of colours, treatments, embossings and prints, made it a designer's dream. Leather became a design material that signified wealth and taste, thereby entrenching its position in the designer market.

Meanwhile, some American designers, including Lisandro Sarasola, North Beach Leather, Francesca Sterlacci, Adrienne Landau, Alicia Herrera and Michael Kors, worked heavily in leather, creating some very interesting techniques, such as Sterlacci's leather lace, Sarasola's leather painting and Landau's woven fur and leather scarves.

Claude Montana's 1980s bold, shouldered black leather jacket was paired with a black leather full skirt, capturing the 'touch girl' image for which the designer is still remembered.

Those designers who used smaller lamb and goat suede skins became more adept at engineering cut lines in creative ways, as demonstrated here in Anne Marie Beretta's voluminous coat in 1984. Beretta turned the necessity of creating the garment from small pieces of skin into a design feature, by embellishing each of the seams in red.

Valentino used shearling, dyed yellow, to create a striking flared topper in 1989. The piecing together of the lambskin can be seen clearly on the sleeves.

This striped leather top from Giorgio Armani's 1980 collection also makes a virtue of the necessity to cut from small pieces of skin.

Azzedine Alaïa's suit from 1984 demonstrates how the trademark wide shoulders of the decade were successfully translated into leather, while the use of decorative stitching on the seams again highlight the construction of the skirt, with its fishtail/godet hem, and jacket from small pieces of leather.

The fine leather used to make Emanuel Ungaro's above-the-knee, double-breasted coats from 1985 show how leather can be eased gently to create fullness at the armhole line.

While big name American designers such as Calvin Klein and Oscar de la Renta began dabbling in leather, it was the hip-hop movement of the late 1980s and early 1990s, especially the '8-ball' jacket, that caused the biggest stir. This multi-coloured leather jacket by Michael Hoban, manufactured by North Beach Leather in autumn 1989, with the '8-ball' motif associated with drug slang for crack heroine, was so popular that young people were being shot for their jackets.

Vivienne Westwood explored the sculptural qualities of leather in this bodice and skirt from 1988. Using a number of sources of inspiration, Westwood took a corset and added elbow crash-pads, combining these with a gathered skirt and upper sleeves from the Victorian era in an eclectic mix that is her trademark style.

In the 1990s European designers began working one-on-one with tanneries. Novelty skins became popular as tanneries in Italy and France competed with each other to create unique looks. Italian tanneries, working with Versace and Armani, experimented with new colours, prints and treatments, while French tanneries worked with French designers to create some of the thinnest and most subtle skins ever.

Leading European designers continued to work leather into their collections, even at the couture level. Gucci, previously known for accessories, branched out into the leather clothing market. And while Thierry Mugler created some of the kinkiest leather pieces, often dominatrix-inspired, Jil Sander took a more classic approach to leather design.

When Gucci moved into leather clothing design, they were able to bring all their knowledge of leather to the catwalk, creating this sophisticated pink coat and dress ensemble in 1991.

In 1991, Thierry Mugler brought biker style to the catwalk with this zipped, hooded jacket and carefully constructed trousers, which take advantage of the sculptural qualities of leather to add to the dominatrix effect.

Jil Sander's 1991 black coat is luxurious both in its style and its use of leather.

1992–1993

As the decade progressed, established designers, including Christian Lacroix, began to embrace the use of leather in their collections, while designers new to the fashion scene, such as Azzedine Alaïa and Americans Isaac Mizrahi and Byron Lars, added whimsy to their leather designs.

Nothing in this beautifully crafted jacket from 1992 betrays the fact Christian Lacroix had never used leather before. He even added a more luxurious touch by incorporating a snakeskin trim.

Byron Lars' stylized aviator jacket of 1992, complete with 'wings' on its shearling collar and accessorized with a 'helmet' and goggles, shows how leather can be combined with other fabrics; here a knit trim is used at the hem and cuffs.

Although Azzedine Alaïa is most known for his sexy, curvy, tight-to-the-body designs, in 1993 he took a softer approach with this pale blue suede cropped jacket and trousers. He took particular advantage of the pieced construction to incorporate decorative seams that were laced together.

Isaac Mizrahi's 1992 take-off of Bonnie Cashin's pocketbook jacket of 1973 gave a great sense of fun to what otherwise might have been just another black leather jacket.

Leather can be sexy or classic. While Claude Montana continued to utilize it to create the fashionable silhouette of the day, and Gianfranco Ferre designed classic styles, Gianni Versace used leather to further his reputation for some of the sexiest clothes to hit the catwalk. Fendi, meanwhile, continued to have a prominent position on the catwalk.

Italian designer Gianfranco Ferre, famous for his white architectural blouses, ventured into leather in 1994 with his beautifully cut, high-waisted, cream-coloured suede gaucho trousers.

Claude Montana often added matching accessories to his ensemble. His batwing suede jacket, paired with matching gauntlets, was a huge hit in 1994.

Continuing the safety-pin theme of his 1994 collection, Versace created this contour-hugging black leather cut-out dress, which fitted supermodel Helena Christensen like a corset.

Known for spectacular furs since 1918, Fendi created this burnished, metallic shearling maxi coat in 1995, designed by Karl Lagerfeld.

Some designers, including Fendi, Ann Demeulemeester and Gucci, continued to incorporate leather into their collections, often using its properties to create a perfect fit for an increasingly pared-down silhouette, while others, such as Thierry Mugler, continued to flirt with the 'bad girl' theme.

Belgian designer Ann Demeulemeester created goth magic with her chic, black leather floor-length dress in 1997.

In 1996, Fendi took to the catwalk with a grey and black ombré shearling maxi coat.

Tom Ford created the ultimate 'power suit' for Gucci in 1997, with his broad-shouldered, black leather jacket and skin-tight pencil skirt.

Parisian designer Thierry Mugler used all the sculptural qualities that only a fabric like leather can provide to create this sexy bustier and skirt trimmed with feathers in 1997. Each section of leather was individually stamped to emphasize its contours, while the skirt and sleeves were designed to resemble articulated pieces of armour.

1998–1999

Leather, suede and **shearling** had a slot in almost every European designer's collection during the late 1990s, with Ungaro's luscious grey shearling jacket and Celine's exquisite tan lambskin coat. Marni's pared-down brown leather funnel-neck coat provided a strong contrast.

The generous collar of Ungaro's short shearling jacket from 1998, fastened with a tie belt, makes good use of the wool face of the skin.

Celine's take on the classic trench coat hit the catwalk in 1999, manufactured with luxurious tan lambskin.

Marni showed this pared-down leather coat with a funnel neck in 1999.

THE TWENTY-FIRST CENTURY

With the turn of the new millennium, designers took leather to a higher level of creativity, inspired by new treatments, such as glazing, distressing, laser cutting, embossing and burnishing, and new metallic colours.

2000

Ann Demeulemeester's floor-length glazed leather dress created high drama on the catwalk in 2000, Dolce & Gabbana featured a tan crocodile embossed coat and Alexander McQueen's show-stopping laser-cut dress caused a sensation. Belgian designer Josephus Thimister created a long and luxurious shearling coat that used skins with a metallic burnished treatment.

Demeulemeester's long dress with gathered waist shows the ability of leather to drape, while the suede detailing at the neckline creates a contrast with the glazed black leather.

Dolce & Gabbana used classic lines for their long tan coat, allowing the embossed crocodile pattern of the leather to create the impact.

Alexander McQueen used laser cutting to create a specially crafted pattern that follows the cut of this buff-coloured dress with its zigzag hem.

This burnished metallic shearling coat by Josephus Thimister is simple in its overall shape, relying on the seams joining the cut skins to create pattern. Instead of disguising natural 'faults' in the skins, Thimister has retained them, adding to the tactile qualities of the coat.

2001

Distressed leather, reminiscent of World War II bomber jackets, made a comeback, this time with a twist, in a 2001 sleeveless trench dress by Italian manufacturer Bally. Laser technology became more popular and designer Jean-Paul Gaultier went a step further with his laser-cut shearling coat. Some designers combined leather with other materials – Valentino created a brown leather and wool trouser suit. Less expensive skins continued to flood the market, and many moderately-priced clothing manufacturers took advantage of this to add panache to their collections.

Jean-Paul Gaultier used laser cutting to emphasize the construction of the back of this fine shearling coat and to create a decorative hemline.

Translating the styling of a trench coat into leather, Bally used distressed leather to echo the military origins of this sleeveless design.

Leather and wool, both natural materials, work particularly well together in this trouser suit by Valentino, the simplicity of the cut foiled by the pattern of the wool.

2002

While Ferragamo lived up to its hallmark values of craftsmanship and superb design, creating classic styles, Julien McDonald for Givenchy and Alexander McQueen emphasized the sexiness of leather, adding a touch of understated raunchiness. Meanwhile, John Galliano sought out traditional uses of leather to create an over-the-top Native American-inspired ensemble.

John Galliano decorated the seams with exaggerated stitches and used bone buttons to add a hint of the handmade to this shearling jacket. The use of rosettes to decorate the sleeves and skirt adds to the Native American theme.

Ferragamo, an Italian company whose reputation in the shoe business dates back to the late 1800s, began creating leather clothing in the 1970s, using only the finest Italian leathers. Classic in its shape and colouring, this jacket nevertheless shows a fine attention to detailing with a gathered armhole, the construction of which has been exposed, and through which a leather tie is threaded. The jacket is accessorized with a stamped leather belt.

Givenchy's close-fitting tan leather trousers have additional snakeskin buckled closures at the waist. Reinforcing at the knees provides an opportunity to add apparently decorative bands of stitching.

Alexander McQueen used a leather belt, shoulder straps and thigh-high leather boots to add to the sexiness of his black corset with lace detail.

Shearling continued to feature on the catwalk with styles by
British Matthew Williamson and American Zac Posen, the former
borrowing from the Native American tradition, the latter from World
War II. Meanwhile, established designers Roberto Cavalli and
Michael Kors both explored embellished and decorative leathers.

*Since the 1960s Roberto Cavalli,
known for the sexy edge of his
collections, has built a reputation
on luxury leathers. This is
demonstrated in this multi-coloured
leather top with decorative corset-
like lines of stitching, paired with
skintight brown leather trousers
and purple leather opera gloves.*

*American designer Michael
Kors, whose name is mostly
associated with classic looks,
used grey marbled leather and
then embellished the edges
with metal ornaments for this
zipped coat.*

The World War II flying suit inspired this shearling jumpsuit by Zac Posen. Made from distressed leather, reflecting its wartime inspiration, it is cleverly cut and constructed so that the seams add to the detailing.

Pocahontas provided the theme for this shearling coat by Matthew Williamson. The pattern is painted on the skin, in the Native American tradition, and is decorated with sequins.

2004

Designers have always sought out anything new and different, and in 2004 animal prints and exotic skins took centre stage. Dolce & Gabbana designed a black patent eelskin jacket, which they paired with a rabbitskin skirt. Other designers working solely in leather, including Hermès and Jordan Betten of Lost Art, both created original designs for their clients that reflect their chosen niche markets – in the case of Betten, the traditional association of leather with music, particularly rock-and-roll. Meanwhile, Alexander McQueen looked to the future with his use of **trapunto**.

The black patented eelskin, with its many painstakingly pieced-together seams, adds a touch of luxury to this ensemble. It is complemented by the rabbitskin skirt, which has been printed with a cheetah pattern. Both were created by Dolce & Gabbana in 2004.

Alexander McQueen had a futuristic design moment when he created this space-age trapunto leather jacket in 2004.

Jordan Betten of Lost Art captured the eye of high-profile celebrities with his rock star leather fashion and his unique design philosophy. His made-to-measure leather clothing and accessories are never sewn by machine. Instead, each seam is sewn by hand with a labour-intensive hand-lacing technique. Betten refuses to sell to retail stores, therefore guaranteeing exclusivity. Rock star Sheryl Crow is seen here wearing leather trousers with feather trim and Betten's trademark handstitched seams.

2005

Established fashion houses Bottega Veneta and Hermès continued to offer interesting leather fashion; they both took the trench to a new level with their tan leather 'trenchsuit', a combination trench coat and jumpsuit. American manufacturer D-Squared and designer Rick Owens used leather to reinterpret their signature looks, D-Squared with their hip orange leather trousers and Rick Owens with his edgy shearling cropped jacket.

Primarily known for their hand-woven leather accessories, Bottega Veneta created this stunning maize leather trench coat in 2005.

D-Squared have taken full advantage of the tanner's craft, producing a pair of hip-hugging orange leather cropped trousers, featuring zipped and patch pockets.

Hermès continued their
creation of innovative
pieces with this melding
of the trench coat and
trouser suit in fine
leather that features
decorative topstitching.

Rick Owens' shearling
jacket with asymmetric
hem shows how colour
variations between two
leather skins can be
used to advantage.

2006

Designers continued to make inventive use of leather. Karl Lagerfeld, who had begun to transform the Chanel image in 1983, showcased just how far he had come when he paired a black leather micro-mini skirt and over-the-knee leather boots with a classic Chanel jacket. John Galliano, always a big fan of leather, included an off-white shearling jacket in his collection for Dior. In keeping with their tradition of experimentation, Dolce & Gabbana combined smooth blue **nappa** with blue-embossed ostrich leather for a military-inspired jacket.

John Galliano's shearling jacket for Dior makes interesting use of darts to provide a decorative touch.

Karl Lagerfeld has contrasted two classic Chanel styles, using black leather for a micro-mini skirt teamed with a cream wool pearl-trimmed jacket. By adding a long chiffon waistcoat and leather knee-high boots, he has further subverted the ensemble.

Dolce & Gabbana show how more exotic leathers, such as ostrich, can be used to give texture to a military-style jacket.

2007

Today's newest designers take leather to another level by creating ultra-mini, sexy, yet playful leather dresses, as here in the example by London-based Christopher Kane from his autumn/winter 2007 collection. Leather legends, including Vuitton, Miu Miu and MaxMara, on the other hand, continue to provide their customers with leather 'classics with a twist'; the twist being leather wardrobe accents that include the ultimate leather belted tunic from MaxMara, a leather flared skirt from Miu Miu and a leather top and shirt ensemble from Vuitton.

Glasgow-born designer Christopher Kane veered away from his signature bondage look into a world of leather and velvet, creating this burgundy ensemble in 2007.

Famous for their coats and suits since 1951, MaxMara ventured into the world of ready-to-wear, with this beautiful brown sleeveless leather tunic in 2007.

Miu Miu treated leather like fabric in 2007 with this full leather front-pleated skirt paired with a matching short leather jacket.

Marc Jacobs used the thinnest, softest leather to create this rust-coloured ensemble in 2007 for Vuitton.

2008

Designers continued to have their own individual take on the use of leather in their collections. Many also exploited the vast range of finishes offered by tanneries, while others created their own leather 'fabrics', using plaiting and weaving techniques. Richard Chai used shearling to create a collection of experimental shapes, while Jordan Betten continued to take a walk on the wild side. Remaining true to his design philosophy, Betten created one-of-a-kind pieces that took more than 100 hours to complete. Meanwhile, French designer Jean Claude Jitrois, one of the first to include stretch leather in his collection, thus eliminating the baggy knee and saggy bottom often associated with skin-tight leather clothing, continued to include the fabric in his collections. Hermès played on its original tradition of horse-riding wear for its new leather line.

Jordan Betten created this top entirely from fine strips of leather, using a combination of weaving and knotting. The use of handcrafted techniques ensures his clients exclusivity of design and manufacture.

Jean Claude Jitrois brought the tuxedo and trousers right up to date in black stretch lambskin.

In the company tradition of making harnesses since 1837, Hermès created these brown suede jodphurs in 2008, to be worn both on and off a horse.

Korean American Richard Chai presented a sleeveless shrug in rust-coloured shearling at his 2008 show.

Although the leather cycle is said to peak every three years, the world's top designers have almost always included leather in their collections. However, leather was especially prevalent on catwalks in 2009. The sophistication of the knee-length skirt by Bally is contrasted with the striking architectural structure of Rick Owens' trousers and top. New York duo Duckie Brown, meanwhile, looked to a classic cut in a striking colour for their soft, luxurious leather jacket.

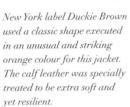

New York label Duckie Brown used a classic shape executed in an unusual and striking orange colour for this jacket. The calf leather was specially treated to be extra soft and yet resilient.

Rick Owens combined an architecturally-cut black leather sleeveless jacket with baggy-style trousers for his 2009 collection.

In 2009, Swiss company Bally showed a tan leather novelty skirt paired with a black halter top.

CHAPTER 2
THE TANNING
PROCESS

Using leather for fashion means investing a considerable amount of effort into turning the raw material into a fabric that is pliable, can be stitched and is wearable. The sensuous nature we associate with leather emerges from the tanning process, and in this chapter we will chart the progress of the raw skin through each stage to the finished aniline or semi-aniline product.

WHAT TANNING DOES

Leather is made by tanneries. A tannery is a factory that buys raw skins, makes the skins into leather, colours the leather and sells it to garment manufacturers.

Leather is animal skin that has been tanned. Tanning does two things to an animal skin:
1. It preserves the skin so that it will not decompose.
2. It adds fats to the hide to make it soft.

THE MAJOR LEATHER MANUFACTURING STEPS

Tanned leather is produced in three distinct stages:

First, a **tannery** must place an order for hides. A tannery can place an order for a particular type or quality of leather requested by an individual garment manufacturer and/or it can place an order anticipating future demand from many different garment manufacturers.

Next, a slaughterhouse (or, as it is often more delicately termed, an **abattoir**) must slaughter an animal and process its hide properly for transport to a tannery. Animals that have been poorly killed or processed will produce poor leather.

The third major stage in leather making is the tanning process itself.

STAGE 1: HOW TANNERIES PURCHASE QUALITY SKINS

In order to make leather, tanneries must first purchase skins from abattoirs. The purchasing process has three stages and is one of the most important aspects of leather making. Tanneries can vary considerably in their raw skin purchasing skills and even the best tanneries cannot make quality leather out of poor-quality raw skins.

The three stages of the leather purchasing process are as follows:

SELECTING THE TYPE OF SKIN TO PURCHASE
The skins from different animals produce very different leathers.

Cowskin is tougher than lambskin, because it is denser and thicker. It can be split into two skins, called **splits**, doubling its yield. For the end user, the top grain side of a split hide is the most expensive to purchase. Only the inside of the split is cheaper.

Pigs have numerous thick-shafted hair follicles, so pig leather is covered with many visible 'dots'. Pigskins can also be split.

Previous spread: Designers using leather today can draw on a wide range of skins and finishes from tanneries across the globe. Here Balenciaga has used a heavy leather with a distressed finish for this zipped jacket from 2000.

Lambskin is the most widely used skin in clothing design. This is because it has an extremely soft 'feel' when tanned properly. However, because lambs are small, their yield per skin is low, resulting in a higher cost per garment. Goat leather can be even softer than lambskin, but its yield is even lower per skin, making it more expensive than lamb.

Leather can be made from just about any animal skin or fish skin. Here are some common leather sources:

Lamb / Salmon / Goat / Peccary / Pig / Python / Shark / Deer / Horse / Cayman crocodile / Elk / Water buffalo / Cow

DECIDING WHERE TO OBTAIN THE SKIN
Most good tanneries have a list of favoured sources, based on years of experience, for almost any type of skin. Yet, when selecting suppliers from their list, they need to keep many geographical factors in mind.

The animal skins used for leather come from all around the world. The quality of skins varies significantly, depending on their source, even among exactly the same animals.

The quality of lambskin, one of the most prized skins in leather making, varies enormously, depending on its country of origin. Most quality tanneries favour lambskins that come from New Zealand or England (**English domestic**). However, very good lambskins can also come from Italy, Iran, Iraq, Spain, India, Pakistan, Australia and the United States.

The country of skin origin is not always a sufficient determinant of skin quality, which can also vary within a country, depending on regional differences in climate and soil quality (which has an impact on the quality of the grass eaten by the animals) and the care provided by different farmers.

Some skins are so rare that they have only a few sources, for example kangaroo, which comes exclusively from Australia, and python, which comes from Africa.

Other speciality skins might come from:

Norway (elk)	**United States (salmon)**
Brazil (peccary)	**Ethiopia (water buffalo)**
Denmark (horse)	**Japan (crocodile)**

DECIDING WHEN TO BUY THE SKIN
The better tanneries know exactly when to purchase skins from a particular location. Even when they don't have orders from garment manufacturers for a particular type of leather, they might purchase the skins anyway, storing them for later use, because they know that there is only one particular time when specific skins should be purchased.

Timing is especially critical when purchasing young animal skins, for example lambskin and vealskin. Since most animals produce their young in a specific period, usually in spring, tanneries need to know exactly when to put in their order for specific hides. This timing will vary by six months between countries south of the equator, where spring starts in October, and countries north of the equator, where spring starts in April.

STAGE 2: HOW ABATTOIRS PROCESS SKINS

KILLING THE ANIMAL

Unfortunately, one of the first steps in creating leather involves the death of an animal. Most animal skin used in leather making comes from abattoirs. These sources invariably use the rest of the animal for food.

The abattoirs in developed countries use very humane methods to kill animals, for example by applying an electrically charged probe to the head of the animal. Most animals are only stunned by the probe, not killed. Once stunned, the animal is often hung by the hind legs. The key arteries are then cut so that the animal bleeds to death.

Tanneries prefer killing methods that do not reduce skin yield. If an animal is agitated by fear or significant physical exercise prior to being stunned and bled, it cannot be fully bled, and random pools of blood will be left in the flesh and skin. This produces bruise marks on the skin, and increases the speed at which the skin will decompose. The bruise marks are known as **cockles** (veins which show up in irregular patterns on a raw skin), and permanently reduce the quality of the skin. The bruises make it impossible for tanneries to colour the skin uniformly.

Although most abattoirs go out of their way to ensure that their animals are calm before the kill, sometimes the quality of the kill cannot be controlled. For example, almost all of the 400,000 deerskins exported from the US are shot by rifle or bow and arrow. These skins will usually be blemished by bullet holes and drag marks and by poor skinning (**flaying**) techniques, often carried out by inexperienced hunters.

From a garment maker's perspective, it is important to note that any blemishes, bruises or other, even seemingly minor, imperfections in a raw hide will be visibly accentuated by the tanning process.

FLAYING THE SKIN

The skin is removed (flayed) from an animal carcass by hand and/ or by machine. First, the butcher (or hunter) makes cuts all around the animal with a sharp knife. The skin is removed by pulling at the skin and using the knife to slice the connective tissue as the skin is pulled. Sometimes the skin itself is cut by mistake.

Sophisticated butchers connect special skinning machines to the ends of cut skin, which then pull the skin off the animal. Skinning machines produce much cleaner, less damaged skins than manual flaying methods.

Generally, hoofed animals are cut straight up and down on their bellies, and the skin is pulled around the (already removed) legs. This protects the valuable skin on the back of the animal from cuts. Exactly the opposite process is used for saurians (crocodiles and lizards), whose bellies are the most important leather sources. These animals are cut along the back first, then skinned towards the front.

After flaying, the skins must be washed immediately in cool water to slow the rotting process.

CURING THE SKIN

Curing is a process that protects skins from rotting. Newly flayed skins should be cured within six hours. At this early stage in the skin production process, only short-term preservation methods are necessary. Generally, abattoirs try to complete all steps leading to the shipment of skins to tanneries within a few weeks.

Rotting, or putrefaction, of the skin is caused by bacteria on the skin. These bacteria produce enzymes, which can liquefy the surface of animal hides. These liquefied portions of hide are then absorbed by the bacteria as food. Any rotted portions of an animal hide will show permanent blemishes, significantly reducing its value to garment makers.

There are three main methods of curing skins: refrigeration, drying and treating with chemicals.

REFRIGERATION

Many abattoirs have freezing or refrigeration facilities. An uncured, refrigerated skin can be stored for about two weeks without damage. Skins can be kept safely for even longer periods of time when frozen. However, freezing can damage the skin if ice crystals form within the skin fibre.

DRYING

Most bacteria need water to survive. Thus, by drying skins thoroughly, most bacteria can't feed normally. When this happens over a prolonged period, some bacteria die, while others revert to a dormant spore form. However, these bacterial spores can quickly revert to hungry bacteria when the skins are rehydrated.

For drying to be effective, skins must contain no more than 10–14 per cent moisture.

Abattoirs usually dry skins by hanging them up outside, although some lay them on the ground to dry in the sun. Since so many skins come from less developed countries with hot, dry climates, air drying is relatively easy and effective. It is more difficult to dry skins in cooler, more northern climates. This is a problem for the abattoirs and tanners in the upper northern or southern hemispheres since, if skins are dried too slowly, they can putrefy before their moisture content drops sufficiently low to stop bacterial action.

CHEMICAL TREATMENTS

Even when water is present, rotting can be slowed or stopped by dissolving certain elements in the water, for example salts, acids, alkalis, bactericides and other toxic chemicals. The most commonly used elements are salts and acids.

Some abattoirs treat skins with special chemicals to prevent rotting. They do this by adding the chemicals to large rotating drums filled with skins.

There are several chemical approaches to preservation. One common approach is to add chemicals that impart a mild acidity level of about 4.5 pH to the skins. This environment is lethal to most bacteria. Another, less toxic, approach to preservation involves immersing the skins in a mildly antiseptic solution of boric acid. These methods of preservation can last from a few days to a few weeks, until the abattoir finds the time to complete the de-hairing and pickling processes.

Salting is the preferred method of preserving skins. To salt skins, abattoirs stack hides, flesh side up, covering each hide thoroughly with coarse grain salt. The amount of salt used to cover the raw hides is generally 25–35 per cent of the weight of the raw hides. The more sophisticated abattoirs immerse newly flayed skins in brine solutions – 1.3 kg (3 lb) salt per 3.8 litres (1 gallon) water – for 12 hours, then they stack the skins. Salting can preserve a skin for months, and for even longer if the skin is dried as well.

DE-HAIRING THE SKIN

Abattoirs must remove the hair on skins prior to transporting them to tanneries.

Some skins, such as lamb, have valuable fur (wool), which has a market value. When the abattoir wishes to sell the fur, the skins are treated with special chemicals so that the fur can be removed by hand without damaging it. First, they immerse the skins in a highly alkaline lime or lye bath to loosen the hair. Then, they pile skins sprayed (on their flesh side) with an acid – usually sulphuric acid – or other chemicals. After 1–2 hours, the chemicals penetrate the skin, allowing abattoir personnel to remove the fur by hand, usually with a special defleshing knife.

When abattoirs do not wish to sell the fur, for example in the case of cowhides, they just throw the skins in a drum containing sulphuric acid, or other chemicals, then rotate the drum until all of the fur is gone.

When most of the hair has been removed, they wash and clean the skins thoroughly to remove lime and any remaining blood, dirt, fur, fat and bacteria. Hunters often use vinegar to neutralize the lime in the skin. This process is called **bating.**

PICKLING

Before storage or transport to tanneries, hairless skins are invariably either pickled or dried, or both. They are usually shipped in a pickled state.

To pickle skins, abattoirs rotate them gently in drums with water, salt and sulphuric acid for about two hours. Although **pickling** stops bacterial activity cold, it will not stop mould growth. Since mould attacks the basic structure of the skin, it can result in uneven dyeing when the skin is eventually tanned. In addition, it can cause a loss of gloss on the finished, tanned skins. To prevent mould, low concentrations of fungicide are added to the pickling solution.

After pickling, the skins are piled into a waterproof container for bulk shipment to tanneries. The stacked pickled lambskins look like piles of thick, wet white paper. Pickled skins can be stored for several months if kept relatively cool.

CRUSTS

A dried raw skin is called a **crust**. Skins are dried into crusts by hanging them in the air in a carefully controlled environment (see Figure 2–1). Many abattoirs ship skins, with or without pickling them, as crusts (see Figure 2–2). Since crusts are so rigid, they are susceptible to cracking or creasing when bent. As a result, they must be carefully tied up, or baled, before shipment to tanneries. Crusts are susceptible to insect attack, so they are often treated with insecticides or poisons, such as arsenic.

FINAL DEFLESHING

Although abattoirs remove most of the animal flesh from their skins before they ship them to tanneries, there will still be white, wispy residues of flesh on the insides of the skins. If the tannery doesn't scrape off all of the flesh before tanning, the tanned skins will have uneven coloration due to poor, irregular penetration of the dyes.

To remove the remaining flesh on a newly purchased skin, a tannery will insert the skins into a shaving machine with rollers at the top and bottom (see Figure 2–3). The machine has a stationary sharp cutting blade very close to the bottom roller. As the skin enters the machine through the two rollers, the blade scrapes the residues of flesh off the skins. Sometimes the shaving is done after the dyeing of the skins if the final weight of the nappa has to be very light, as little as 0.4 mm (1 oz). This is done to prevent the lightweight skins from tearing during the dyeing process in the drums.

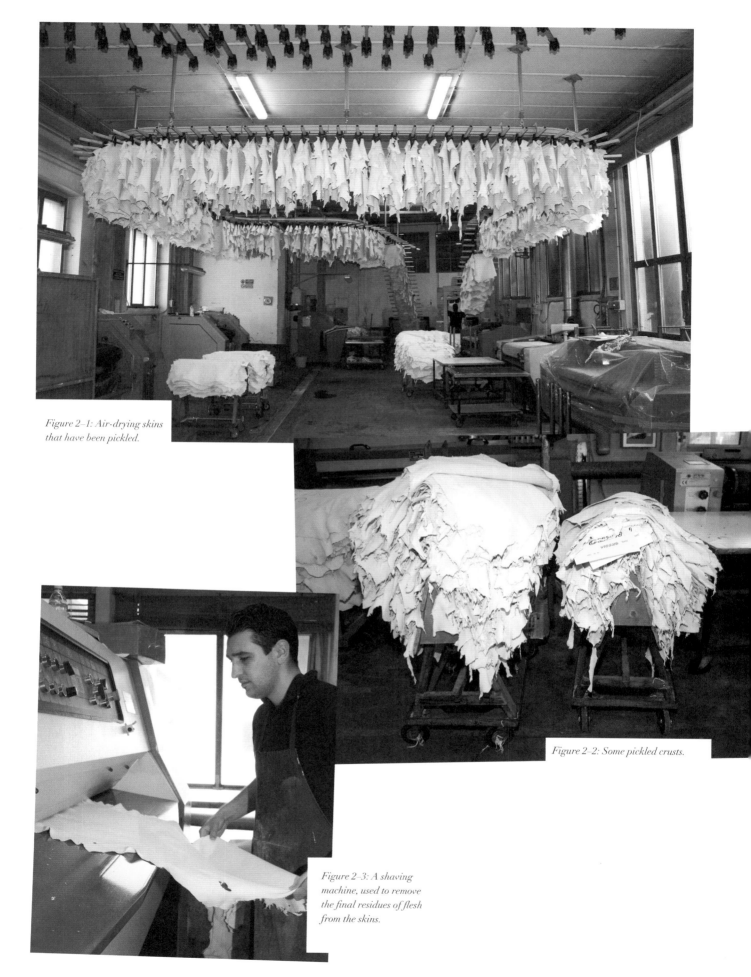

Figure 2–1: Air-drying skins that have been pickled.

Figure 2–2: Some pickled crusts.

Figure 2–3: A shaving machine, used to remove the final residues of flesh from the skins.

STAGE 3: THE TANNING PROCESS

Most quality leather or suede garments are made from lambskin or goatskin, although cowskin can sometimes be more expensive than lamb. Because of the popularity of lambskin, however, we will concentrate on describing the tanning of this skin. However, a very similar process is employed to tan the skins of other animals.

A tannery specializing in lambskin usually receives pickled raw skins from their suppliers. Occasionally, they are delivered as crusts (see page 62). In the latter case, the tannery will soak the crusts in salt water until the skins are thoroughly wet. This brine solution helps to open the pores in the skin for the better penetration of tanning solutions.

There is no way to generalize the tanning process for all skins. Each skin is different and must be treated differently. The specific amount of chrome powder, **basifying agents**, **fat liquor**, waterproofing agents, softeners etc. added to skins during the tanning process varies significantly depending on the animal and the location from where it came.

There is really only one limiting factor in tanning: the quality of the original raw skins. Tanning cannot make a poor quality skin into a great skin. While tanneries can influence certain quality variables (for example, adding more vegetable tannins can make skins drier, or adding more fat liquors can make skins softer), they can't make a skin any drier or softer than its original raw potential allows.

In the next few pages most of the key steps in tanning will be summarized. However, different tanneries execute the tanning

Figure 2–4: The tanning drum.

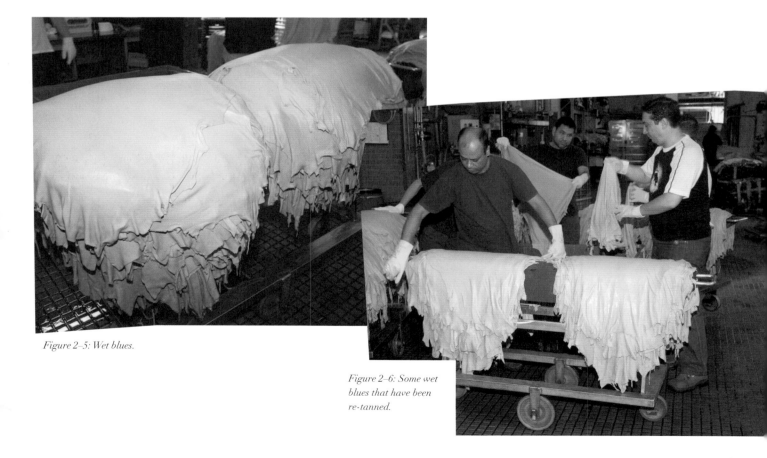

Figure 2–5: Wet blues.

Figure 2–6: Some wet blues that have been re-tanned.

process in different ways. For example, a tannery that specializes in cheap leather for novelty clothing might skip some of the expensive, labour-intensive procedures such as final defleshing (see page 62). In addition, many of the very high quality tanneries utilize expensive secret processes, while the cheaper tanneries try very hard to avoid adding any extra steps to the tanning process.

MAKING WET BLUES

This is really the most important step in tanning. In fact, this is the only step in the entire process that is actually called 'tanning' by the tanneries.

To produce **wet blues**, tanneries place fully defleshed, pickled skins into a large rotating drum (see Figure 2–4). These drums are usually made of wood, look like giant wooden barrels and can hold between 1,000 and 3,000 skins each. Tannery personnel rotate the skins in the drum and add chromium sulphate powder, plus other (often proprietary) ingredients. The skins are rotated in these drums for roughly eight hours.

When the skins come out of the drums, they are light blue in colour (see Figure 2–5). The tannery sets out the newly tanned skins for three days to let the chrome solution seep into the thickest parts of the skins. After tanning, the tanneries usually wash the skins in water to eliminate excess chromium salts.

Chrome is the key element in chromium sulphate. It transforms the natural proteins in a skin to an inert substance that resists rotting. Skins that have been tanned with chrome never lose their tannage, even when soaked in water.

OTHER 'TANNING' INGREDIENTS

In years past, homes and tanneries used vegetable matter to tan skins. This process usually involves boiling tree bark and/or other vegetable matter, until a 'tea' filled with natural vegetable **tannin** is produced. In fact, the term 'tanning' came from the original process of immersing raw skins in a tannin-containing solution. The most common vegetable sources for natural tannins are oak bark, hemlock bark, gambier, terra japonica and various by-products of the wood-processing industry.

RE-TANNING

Some tanneries insert additional steps between tanning and the next wet process, **neutralization**. In this step, the wet blues are processed with special ingredients designed to make the skins lighter, softer or harder, or otherwise produce whatever characteristic is desired by the tannery (see Figure 2–6). For example, if the tannery wants to constrict the fibres of the skins to minimize skin pore size, they might add aluminium-containing powder to the re-tanning drums. Generally, tanneries put the skins designated for re-tanning into the same drums they plan to use for dyeing, not the initial tanning drums.

Figure 2–7: Air-dried crusts, ready for storage until needed.

STORING SKINS FOR LATER USE

Occasionally, a tannery might want to store the fully defleshed, wet blue skins for a while before further processing. This would occur, for example, when the tannery has purchased more skins than it has open manufacturer orders.

To store already tanned skins, the tannery will dry them into crusts. To do this, the tannery first wrings out excess moisture by inserting the skins into a large machine with two long rollers. The machine is called the **setting-out machine**. This wringing out process is called **setting out** the skins.

Following the setting out process, the skins are hung and left to dry for several days in the air. Some tanners have very large drying machines which are 12–18 m (40–60 ft) in length. These tanneries hang their skins on a moving overhead conveyor belt, which transports the hanging skins into and out of the dryer. When the skins exit the dryer, they are fully dried (see Figure 2–7). Crusts can then be stored for several years, even indefinitely, without deterioration.

SORTING AND SELECTING SKINS

The sorting process can occur at any stage during the pre- or post-tanning (wet blues) process. In fact, it usually occurs several times per skin. Even though most tanneries work hard to buy the best possible skins to start with, they still spend a considerable time evaluating, and re-evaluating, the skins they already own.

First, a tannery sorts skins based on their physical quality. During this procedure, trained tannery inspectors examine the crusts on tables. Different skins from the same type of animal may have different physical flaws, for example one animal may have been cut severely by barbed wire during his lifetime, while another may have been poorly flayed by the abattoir or an inexperienced hunter. Still another animal may have cockles (see page 61).

Second, the tannery decides which skins should be made into suede (where the *inside* of the skin will be worn on the outside of a garment) and which skins will be made into nappa (where the *outside*, formerly fur-bearing, side of the skin will be worn on the outside of a garment). They make this determination by carefully examining both the inside and outside (also called **grain side**) of the skins. In a fine tannery, 50 per cent of its output might be nappa and 50 per cent suede. Suede can be made with skins of a relatively lower quality than those used for nappa. Thus, although suede requires a few more processing steps than nappa, it usually costs less to purchase.

NEUTRALIZING

Because wet blues are made from pickled skins, they are quite acidic (2.0–3.0 pH). Before the skins can be passed to the pre-dyeing and dyeing processes, the skins must be made more alkaline (about 5.0 pH). Tanneries add basifying agents to rotating drums containing wet blues to neutralize their acidity.

PREPARATIONS FOR DYEING

Tanneries add other ingredients to the newly tanned skins following the neutralization process. These other ingredients vary, depending upon the type and quality of skins being processed and the experience, traditions, and research and development sophistication of each individual tannery.

The truly mandatory additive is fat liquor. Fat liquors condition (add oils to) the skins. In many ways, this is the most important additive, other than chrome, used in the tanning process, because it returns the skin to its natural softness.

The very best skins will be processed with fat liquors and other ingredients to ready them for becoming **aniline skins**. Aniline skins are pre-processed so that later, during the dyeing process, dyes can penetrate the skin completely from one side to the other. They are so good that they do not require sprayed on, cover-up dyes to hide defects. Aniline skins can be either nappa or suede.

The majority of skins have visible flaws, some minor, others quite visible. These skins must be further processed to become **semi-aniline** nappa. There is really no suede counterpart to this grade, since the semi-aniline process involves spraying skins with coats of dye or plastic film designed to obscure flaws. The merits and demerits of aniline versus semi-aniline skins are discussed later.

The remaining crusts in a tannery's inventory will have flaws so severe that they can be used only for hidden garment linings. Some of these may be printed with designs, to hide their defects.

DYEING THE SKINS

The colour of fine leather is one of its most important attributes. To dye skins, tanneries place them in special dyeing drums (see Figures 2–8 and 2–9). These are not the same drums as the tanning drums used to make the wet blues. The tanneries add special dyes and several other ingredients (often proprietary) to the drums. The dyes usually come from companies specializing in selling tanning supplies.

Most tanneries add the dyes to the drums by hand. Some sophisticated tanneries use computer-controlled, automatic ingredient feeders to add various ingredients to the dye bath in the drums. These sophisticated systems add dyes and other chemicals based on the weight of the skins in the drum.

The skins are wet when they are removed from the drums. They are put on rolling pallets and left to sit for a while to drain off liquids. The tannery will then dry the skins using the setting out process, putting the skins through giant rollers before air drying them.

Some very thin suedes are too delicate for the roller machines. These skins are carefully vacuumed (see Figure 2–10) to suck out the water. Then the skins are air dried in one of two ways:
1. The skins are hung out to dry naturally, or
2. They are moved, via a conveyer device, through a heated, forced-ventilation drying tunnel (see Figure 2–11).

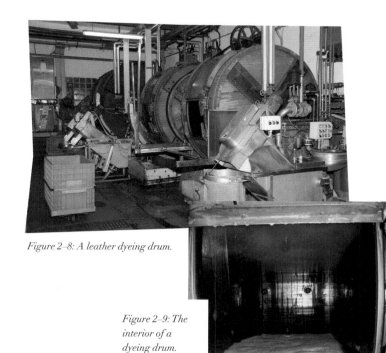

Figure 2–8: A leather dyeing drum.

Figure 2–9: The interior of a dyeing drum.

STAKING

Since the drying process can sometimes shrink skins a bit, the **staking** process seeks to stretch them out to their normal size without re-wetting them.

Not all skins need to be staked, just those that tend to shrink excessively. In principle, all goat- and lambskins need to be staked after drying, while antelope suede, for example, will not need to go through this process as it is dryed on the vacuum dryer and will not shrink. It is difficult to say which skins shrink more or less, as it depends on different factors such as weight and humidity. These factors are determined at the tannery once the tanning process is completed.

There are two main ways to stake leather:
1. Put the leather through giant rollers to flatten it, or
2. Stake it by hand.

For high-volume staking, most tanneries use high-volume staking machines (see Figure 2–12.) These work much like setting-out machines, by pulling the skins through two rollers, flattening them into slightly resilient (but mostly still rigid) pancakes. At the end of this phase, the edges of the crust are no longer upturned.

Some tanneries stake their higher quality, smaller skins the old-fashioned way, by hand. They might use any one of various machines to assist them in their objective, but the effort they put into each skin involves highly skilled manual labour.

Most of the hand-staking operations involve machines of some sort. However, unlike the high-volume staking machines, which literally roll over the whole skin in one pass, the hand-staking machines stake only one small part of the skin's surface during each pass of the device.

A typical hand-staking machine has a large wheel, almost the size of a narrow car tyre, which rotates away from the machine's operator. Each wheel has scores of dull blades on it, each running from left to right. The machine operator takes a skin, holds the two width-side edges of the skin with both hands and, while stretching the skin between both hands, presses it against the rotating wheel of the machine.

This operation is repeated over and over again until all surfaces on the skin have been staked to the operator's satisfaction.

Although this process costs significantly more than the high-volume method, the better tanneries routinely hand stake their leathers, using different, highly specialized machines or different wheel surfaces to produce differences in appearance and/or softness in their more expensive products.

Figure 2–10: Vacuum-drying some suede skins.

Figure 2–11: Air-drying dyed nappa skins.

Figure 2–12: Staking by machine.

FINISHING TOUCHES

Throughout the centuries, tanneries around the world have developed their own tanning and finishing techniques; techniques that set them apart from their competition. These proprietary techniques are often well-guarded secret recipes and include making a skin softer, shinier, more glazed, polished or buffed, plumper, less or more stretchy, distressed or with any number of other unique characteristics.

As an example, if a tannery wanted to produce an aniline nappa leather with a particularly shiny surface, it might stake the leather using an old, one-of-a-kind 'glazing' machine. These machines are often designed and created by the tanneries themselves (see Figure 2–13.)

One top-quality tannery in Italy has a custom-made machine, which repeatedly rolls a small 13-cm (5-inch) glass roller over the skins, using extremely heavy pressure. The machine's operator must constantly move the skin by hand underneath the ever-rolling glass roller until the entire skin has been rolled. Because the whole process is done by hand, any areas on the skin that require it will get an extra press from the glass roller.

The glazing process results in a totally uniform, naturally shiny leather product, without the somewhat artificial, sprayed-on shininess resulting from the semi-aniline process.

The suede polishing machine (see Figure 2–14) polishes the suede side of a skin to produce a nice nap, a kind of 'writing effect'. To remove any remaining unwanted dust in the suede, each skin is passed through a de-dusting machine (see Figure 2–15). To achieve a shine rather than a glaze, a nappa skin will be passed through an ironing machine (see Figure 2–16).

Figure 2–14: A suede polishing machine.

Figure 2–15: A suede de-dusting machine.

Figure 2–13: A glazing machine, used to produce an optimum product.

Figure 2–16: An ironing machine.

GRADING THE SKINS

Tanneries decide well in advance of dyeing their skins whether the skins will be aniline or semi-aniline.

After staking, the potential aniline skins are separated from the rest of the skins. They are graded at this point as being either A, B or C quality. Naturally, 'A' quality aniline skins earn the tannery more money than B or C quality skins. The better tanneries produce 50 per cent A, 30 per cent B and 20 per cent C quality aniline skins. As a garment maker, though, you need to understand that these quality grades are based on the tannery's own judgement. Keep in mind that the tannery's natural inclination will be to upgrade, not downgrade, a skin's quality grade. Some designers joke that tanneries seem to produce 95 per cent A quality skins and 5 per cent B quality skins on a consistent basis. If you find yourself buying lots of aniline skins in the future, you would be wise to visit tanneries and pick what you yourself consider to be A quality.

Tanneries will do a final trimming of each skin as they check, grade and sort them (see Figure 2–17). The skins are then moved to an electronic measuring machine (see Figure 2–18) where they are stamped on the back with a number representing their area. After this, the skins are rolled and bundled for shipment to customers (see Figures 2–19 and 2–20).

Figure 2–18: A skin measuring machine.

Figure 2–19: Rolling the skins.

Figure 2–17: The final trimming and sorting of skins.

Figure 2–20: Some rolled and bundled skins.

SPRAY TREATMENTS

Any skin that has undergone any sort of surface treatment, whether it involves spraying on extra coats of dye, or merely a clear plastic film, is called a semi-aniline skin. Most skins purchased by even the very best tanneries have sufficiently serious physical defects to require spraying to hide surface flaws. A few years ago, a typical tannery would just as soon have produced only aniline skins, very soft skins without any sprayed-on additives, because it could sell each of these skins for much more money than a semi-aniline skin. In today's market, however, many manufacturers actively seek out good semi-aniline skins. In fact, a really good semi-aniline skin may not even look noticeably different from an aniline skin, which will have been processed with water-repelling chemicals during the tanning process.

Semi-aniline skins are often less expensive than aniline skins. However, they do not usually have the soft feel and subtle coloration of aniline skins. On the other hand, since they are often protected by sprayed-on chemicals, they are usually much more resistant than aniline skins to water and other spills.

Tanneries prepare semi-aniline skins by using two giant machines, a spraying machine and a drying machine. The skins are placed flat on wide conveyer belts, two to three skins wide. The belts move the skins into a spraying machine. This machine has four to six air pressure-controlled spray nozzles, each connected to a central hub located above the flat skins, which rotate at 50–60 rpm. As the skins pass below the rotating nozzles, the machine sprays dyes or other chemicals onto the skins (see Figure 2–21).

After the skins have been sprayed, they move immediately into a drying machine, which is always physically connected to the spraying machine. The drying machine uses steam heat and forced ventilation (fans) to dry the skins during the minute or so it takes the conveyer belts to move them through the machine.

The spraying and drying steps are usually repeated several times. The tanneries make this simple by stringing together several pairs of sprayers and dryers, all fed by the same wide conveyer belt. Since these machines are quite large, a large string of, say, five pairs of sprayers and dryers might be up to 40–46 m (130–150 ft) in length. Usually, the number of sprayer/dryer pairs linked together ranges between three and five. A typical tannery will almost always have at least two separate spraying lines.

The tanneries spray two different types of ingredients onto semi-aniline skins. First, they might spray several additional coats of dye onto the skin to cover up imperfections. Second, they might spray different films onto the skins to give them specific qualities, depending on customer requests, for example to make the surface of a skin more glossy, or to waterproof a skin.

For very high quality semi-aniline skins (but still not of sufficiently high quality to make them pure aniline), tanneries may try to limit their spray treatments to one coat of clear plastic film, either to waterproof or to shine up the surface of a skin. Even these mostly clear spray additives will conceal minor blemishes and discoloration on the skins.

Remember, there is always one unfortunate, but unavoidable, result of spraying skins. They will lose some of their softness. A skin sprayed even once, with a very light film or dye, will always be noticeably harder to the touch than equal quality, unsprayed skins.

In general, while you should probably rate semi-aniline skins lower than aniline skins made from equal quality hides, you should be aware that many well-made semi-aniline skins can be breathtakingly beautiful and are virtually indistinguishable from aniline skins. They can also be just as expensive as, or even more expensive than, aniline skins. They may very well be a better choice for your garment design than aniline skins.

Figure 2–21: Spraying a skin.

DECORATIVE TECHNIQUES

Tanneries create unique decorative techniques for embellishing leather skins. One of the most popular is embossing. Metal embossing plates (see Figure 2–22) containing patterns that mimic alligator, crocodile, ostrich, rhinoceros, elephant or other rare, endangered or extinct birds, reptiles, amphibians and mammals, are placed in special embossing machines (see Figure 2–23). Skins are fed individually into the machine, resulting in an all-over patterned skin that is often indistinguishable from the authentic version.

Other decorative options include foil overlays that create metallic skins in every colour imaginable when heat and pressure are applied. A heavy film overlay can be used to create patent leather. Skins can be printed to resemble fabric or they can be laundered or distressed for an antique or vintage look. Laser cutting creates intricate patterns resembling lace, while leather plaiting weaves leather into 'cloth', to add yet another dimension. Quilting, appliqué and embroidery, as well as bonding lycra knit to the back to create 'stretch leather', add to leather's versatility. Some designers work directly with tanneries to develop exclusive techniques that give them a competitive advantage, while others create their own embellishments, such as patchwork, smocking, lacing, hand-tooling, tie-dyeing, painting and crocheting. Applying studs, stones, fringing, beads or other objects simply adds to the wonderful allure of leather.

Figure 2–23: An embossing machine.

Figure 2–22: Embossing plates, used to produce a patterned skin.

CHAPTER 3
THE DESIGN
PROCESS

This chapter will outline the techniques that a designer might employ to design a leather and faux leather collection. Naturally, one cannot define exactly how a designer should approach the creative process, and many of the great designers approach the design process in quite different ways.

DESIGN INSPIRATION

Clothing design usually begins with an inspiration. Inspiration can be the material itself or a person, place or thing.

The key attribute of a designer is to be constantly curious and observant of the world around you. To design collection after collection, bringing originality and style to a range of garments, requires an outward focus. Good places to start are trend shows, museums and libraries, and observing current cultural themes.

DEFINE YOUR CUSTOMER

If you are to design affordable, desirable clothes you will need to know the age and socio-economic profile of your customer. If your customer is young, you will want to design trendy, fun and affordable clothes, so you will have to pay particular attention to the price of the skins that you select for your design. Similarly, if you have an older, more mature customer, you may want to design a more conservative or classic garment, with attention paid to interesting details. You must always choose your skins according to your price point.

GO SHOPPING

Market research is the best way to see, at first hand, what the competition is doing as well as to learn what your customer is buying. It also gives you the opportunity to see the types of skins being used by other designers, the silhouettes that are being shown for that season and what the price points are.

ATTEND FORECAST/TREND SHOWS

Most designers, especially those in the mass market category, will want to know what fashion industry trend services are predicting for the upcoming season. While there are no trend services exclusively for leather apparel, forecast services, such as Peclers, Promostyl and the Doneger Group, provide information that can be used by leather apparel manufacturers. These services predict colour, fabric, silhouette and trend information, for a membership fee. Fibre manufacturers Cotton Incorporated and DuPont offer trend and colour information at no charge. See Resources at the back of this book for more information about these services.

ATTEND TRADE SHOWS

There are numerous leather shows throughout the year. These shows allow designers to keep abreast of the latest trends and advances in leather tanning and design. New treatments, colours and skin textures are always being introduced at these shows. Leather designers should also keep up to date on textile trends by attending the top fabric shows, such as Premier Vision in Paris (October and March) and the International Fabric Fashion Fabric Exhibition in New York (November and April).

Previous spread: Enrico Cavalli turns up the heat with his bustier jumpsuit, complete with sexy cut-outs, made using metallic leather.

TRAVEL TO FIND INSPIRATION

Many mass manufacturers find inspiration in New York, Los Angeles, Paris, Amsterdam, London, Milan, Florence, Munich, Düsseldorf, Montreal, Tokyo, Barcelona and Brussels. Their designers might photograph merchandise in store windows, sketch things that they see and/or purchase items that they might wish to copy or interpret for their own collection. This is a way for their company management to see new merchandise and trends at first hand.

READ TRADE PRESS

Designers should constantly read fashion magazines for colour and trend direction. See Resources for a listing of the top magazines. In addition to the specialized leather apparel magazines, designers should read all of the most important fashion magazines, both American and European, such as *Vogue*, *Harper's Bazaar*, *Elle*, *Marie Claire*, *L'Uomo*, *Collezioni*. Designers should also regularly read trade papers such as *Women's Wear Daily* for up-to-the-minute information. Designers affiliated with a manufacturer who is a member of the Leather Industries of America or the Leather Apparel Association, should also be reading the newsletters produced by these trade organizations for current information.

CARRY OUT RESEARCH IN MUSEUMS AND LIBRARIES

Designers can gain inspiration from numerous sources but one of the best ways comes from studying what designers in the past have done. Many museums throughout the world, including the Victoria & Albert Museum in London, the Metropolitan Museum of Art and the Museum at the Fashion Institute of Technology (FIT) in New York, exhibit the costumes of particular designers and/or certain periods in history, which can have a surprising influence on current fashion trends. FIT in New York also has wonderful exhibits and a very extensive costume library, as does the Musée de la Mode in Paris. All of these museums and institutes also have book and magazine libraries.

PAY ATTENTION TO NON-FASHION EVENTS AND TRENDS

Designers should always be aware of *all* of the events that are going on around them. Current trends in music, film, dance, theatre and even local news can be potential sources of design inspiration. Some of the major trends in fashion in the past have been a result of such influences. For example, many designers have tied their collections into musical trends such as grunge and hip-hop. 'People watching' from a park bench or from a table at a street café can also provide inspiration.

Ralph Rucci begins his design process with a series of sketches. Here, designs for spring 2009 are pinned up in his workroom showing a 'Miza' jacket, in white double-faced crepe on silk tulle, and a kimono with a fitted torso in vibration double-faced crepe on silk tulle.

Rucci's skilled artisans are able to transform his ideas into leather 'fabric'. For autumn 2008, he created a feather dress with a braided, leather samurai bodice.

Rucci created this braided leather jacket as a japanese basket over a boiled white chiffon blouse and bias silk/wool hammered satin trousers.

Rucci found inspiration in the work of artist Louise Nevelson for his warm-up suit in black georgette with matt-brown alligator paillettes to mimic ribbing, from his haute couture 2006 collection.

ORGANIZING AND PLANNING YOUR COLLECTION

Once you have followed these steps, you should have enough information to begin organizing and planning your collection. By focusing on the fashion interests and economic means of your customer, you should have a very good idea of what you need to create.

Jordan Betten of Lost Art is an example of a designer who caters to a high-profile clientele. Betten claims that his collection is 'inspired by the materials themselves, the ceremonial and primitive form of dress that is intertwined with rock and roll and my life'. His handmade, custom leather clothing is worn by celebrities such as Sheryl Crow, Steven Tyler, Lenny Kravitz and Britney Spears.

Having done your research, you should know what skins will be important in the coming season. You should establish a colour story by selecting two to six colours (per skin quality) that you think will best complement the line.

For larger, more mass market-oriented companies, one of the best ways to organize your thoughts and ideas is to create a theme or inspiration board. Later, you will also want to create a style board. These will help you to visualize the line and to present concepts to your manufacturer's sales staff and retail buyers.

The combination of theme board and style board can be very cost-effective, since both will help you and your manufacturer to determine the viability of a line concept before initiating the very expensive process of sample making.

CREATE A MOOD BOARD

A **mood board** (also called a concept or theme board) is a visual presentation designed to communicate the general concept or mood you believe will help you to sell your line to the target customer.

Most are made up of a collage of photographs, tear sheets or photocopies from books or magazines. Boards can be computer-generated from scanned images, printed out and mounted on 5-mm (¼-inch) foam core board. Typically, the dimensions of the foam core board are either 50 x 75 cm (20 x 30 inches) or 75 x 100 cm (30 x 40 inches).

The photos, photocopies and tear sheets should complement your colour story and you should use artist's materials to make the best possible impression. When you present your board, your audience will be several metres away, so your visual materials need to be big enough for everyone in the audience to see them from a distance. Always choose the strongest visuals possible, so that your board makes a strong and immediate impression.

Make sure you include the following:
1. One or two photographs of the target customer – it is important to describe exactly who is going to buy your final product.
2. Between three and five images that depict your recommended theme or convey the 'mood' you are trying to create – make sure that these visuals are meaningful and not vague.
3. Recommended trims or other objects – if a certain button style captures the gist of your idea, attach a few to the board. If you want to convey a military feel, include a real epaulette and some medals.

Andrew Marc, a division of GIII Apparel Group, based their autumn 2009 collection on three different inspirations: sleek machines, high-button boot buttons reminiscent of M&Ms, and things that are 'curly'. Images were used to reinforce the target market, in this case the sexy 25–50-year-old woman who is urban but not avant-garde. The colours used in all three groups were black, brown, deep red and metallic silver, copper and gunmetal, in keeping with the brand's DNA of 'trendy' but not 'fashion victim'.

TIPS FOR MAKING AN INTERESTING MOOD BOARD

There are many ways to approach the design of a mood board. Here are some specific ideas for ensuring that your board is interesting and effective:
1. Plan the layout carefully. Experiment with placing your photographs, tearsheets, swatches and other materials in different positions on the board until you achieve the best result. Your theme board should be visually exciting and, of course, it must be able to get your 'message' across effectively.
2. You may also want to include some swatches of your recommended skins. Make sure that these are sufficiently large for your intended audience to be able to distinguish their individual characteristics. They should not be smaller than 5 x 7 cm (2 x 3 inches). You can create a three-dimensional quality by occasionally folding and/or artfully arranging your swatches. If using patterned or printed skins, make sure your swatches are large enough to show the complete pattern effectively. Sometimes designers mount their swatches on the board with Velcro®. This makes it easier for the members of your audience to remove the swatches for detailed inspection.

Jordan Betten (centre, wearing hat) and his workers create intricate one-off pieces, valued by his high-profile customers for their exclusivity.

Betten lists record covers, beads and the leather itself among his sources of inspiration.

Over the last ten years Betten has acquired a clientele that includes many rock stars and musicians.

DESIGNING AND MERCHANDISING YOUR COLLECTION

Designers initiate the design process in different ways. Some begin with the silhouette while others are inspired by a particular skin or material. Most designers do rough sketches first. Once they feel comfortable with a particular direction, they focus on perfecting those that they think will work. Some designers will mount all of their rough sketches on a wall or some corkboard before beginning the editing process.

One theme board variation from Andrew Marc (see page 79), is on sliding panels so that ideas can be easily removed and added. Note the use of 'props' to communicate the message – zip swatches, high button boot samples and shearling swatches.

MERCHANDISING YOUR COLLECTION

A good designer will merchandise individual styles in appropriate groups, taking care to create balance within each group. For instance, a balanced line of outerwear will include a range of styles within each group, such as short jackets, medium length coats, three-quarter length coats and long coats. The line will also include a balanced assortment of collar treatments, such as notched, fur-trimmed, banded and hooded.

The merchandising objective behind the creation of well-balanced groups is to maximize your sales by motivating a buyer to buy several styles within a group. For example, if you only offer a buyer a range of short jackets, then he or she will concentrate on deciding which *one* of those short jackets to buy. If you offer several groups, each consisting of one short jacket, one three-quarter length coat and one long coat, the buyer will tend to concentrate on deciding which whole *group* of three styles to buy. By presenting a balanced collection, you are more likely to get three sales out of each buyer instead of only one.

The same principles apply to merchandising sportswear. However, here you will often want to balance each group by offering a variety of looks and combinations.

STYLE BOARD

The style board can also include flat sketches of all of the styles in a particular theme. Generally, the sketches show both the front and back views of each garment. The sketches should be large enough to see details of each garment, and never smaller than 7.5 x 10 cm (3 x 4 inches) each. However, style boards sometimes depict styles on a fashion figure for a more dramatic effect.

For large collections, designers generally prepare both a theme board and a style board to present their design concepts fully. For smaller groups, many designers combine their theme and style boards.

In either case, the style board should depict:
1. The target customer.
2. The featured skin.
3. The colour story.
4. The mood.
5. The styles offered in the line.

A collection that is well researched, designed and presented with theme and style boards can ensure increased sales and reduced costs. The boards act as organizational tools for designers, selling platforms for sales people and merchandising aids for buyers. They can also prevent a manufacturer proceeding with a poorly conceived line, wasting precious production time and making expensive samples.

THE REMAINING STEPS IN THE DESIGN PROCESS

Once the best styles have been approved for sample making, the process is as follows:
1. The pattern maker makes the pattern.
2. The sample maker sews a muslin or canvas prototype.
3. The designer fits the muslin and makes any necessary corrections.
4. The sample maker cuts and sews the garment using production skins.
5. The designer fits the final sample and makes any additional adjustments.

When a company manufactures overseas, once the garment has been approved for sample making, the process is as follows:
1. The designer completes a design/spec sheet which specifies everything the overseas sample maker needs to know about the design, including exactly which skin or skins to use.
2. The overseas factory will follow the design/spec sheet and send the sewn sample made up in the specified skin.
3. The designer will fit and inspect the garment and tell the overseas factory what corrections need to be made.
4. The overseas factory will continue to revise the garment until the designer is happy with it.

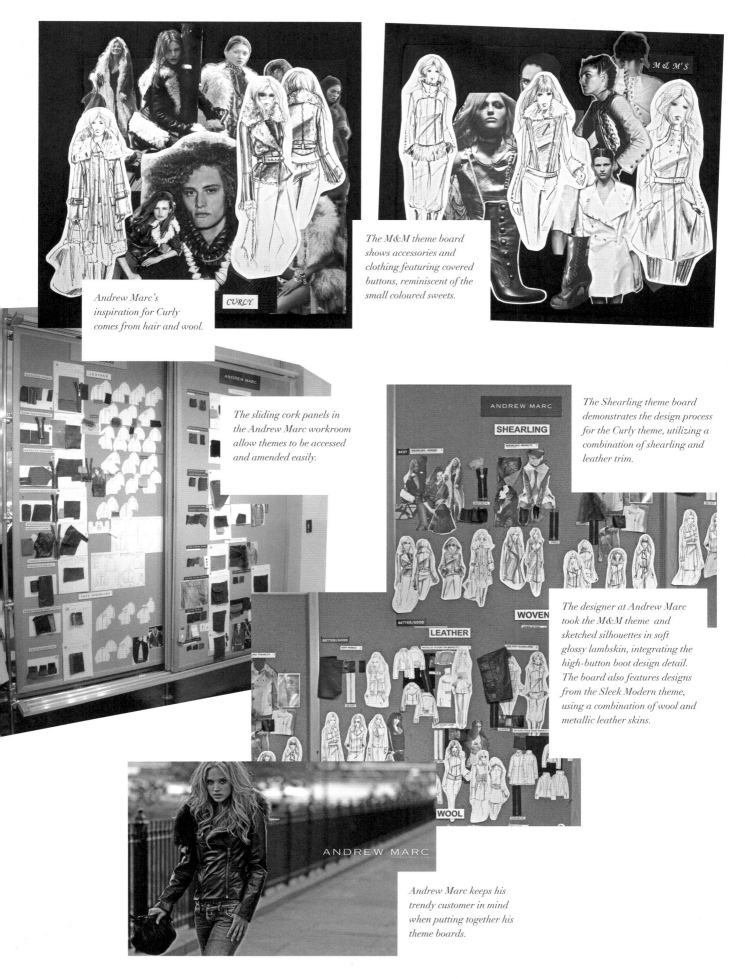

Andrew Marc's inspiration for Curly comes from hair and wool.

The M&M theme board shows accessories and clothing featuring covered buttons, reminiscent of the small coloured sweets.

The sliding cork panels in the Andrew Marc workroom allow themes to be accessed and amended easily.

The Shearling theme board demonstrates the design process for the Curly theme, utilizing a combination of shearling and leather trim.

The designer at Andrew Marc took the M&M theme and sketched silhouettes in soft glossy lambskin, integrating the high-button boot design detail. The board also features designs from the Sleek Modern theme, using a combination of wool and metallic leather skins.

Andrew Marc keeps his trendy customer in mind when putting together his theme boards.

CHAPTER 4
PLANNING

You should keep a number of things in mind when you design in leather or suede. The most important consideration is: what type of skin will most enhance the design I have in mind? In this chapter we will look at the characteristics of different types of leather, how to choose the right leather for your design, and then how to plan your pattern to make the best use of the skin.

HAND

Just like any woven fabric, leather can be obtained in a wide range of textures and qualities, partly dependent on the original skin and partly, as we have seen, on the tanning and finishing techniques through which it has been passed. Selecting the right leather is key to the design.

The overall feel of a skin, its stiffness or softness, is known as its **hand**. Just as you would choose a soft fabric to create a drapey blouse, you would choose a soft lamb suede to create a wonderfully soft, sexy suede shirt. Similarly, if you want to create a tight-fitting skirt with a lot of stitching detail, you may want to select a stiffer skin, such as pig suede.

WEIGHT

The **weight** of a skin is closely related to its hand. Skins vary in weight from animal to animal. The weight of a skin is defined as the number of oz (kg) per 1 sq ft (0.092 sq m) of skin. Generally, 1 sq ft of leather weighing 1 oz (0.028 kg) tends to be about 0.4 mm (1/64 inch) thick. If you order a '2-oz skin (0.056-kg)', you'll generally get a skin that's about 0.8 mm (1/32 inch) thick – twice as thick as a '1-oz' skin. Most vendors will talk in terms of millimeters instead of fractions of inches. Table 4–1 provides conversion estimates of weight to thickness:

TABLE 4–1 LEATHER THICKNESS BY WEIGHT

INCHES	MM	WEIGHT kg (oz)
1/64	0.4	0.02 (1)
1/32	0.8	0.05 (2)
3/64	1.2	0.08 (3)
1/16	1.6	0.011 (4)
5/64	2.0	0.014 (5)
3/32	2.4	0.017 (6)
7/64	2.8	0.019 (7)

Here are some simple rules of thumb for determining weights and thicknesses for odd measurements:

TABLE 4–2 'ODD' MEASUREMENTS

0.1 mm = 7g (¼ oz)

1.0 mm = 70.8g (2½ oz)

You will almost never have to use skins heavier than 2½ oz (1 mm) in garment making. The typical leather shirt will be about 1¼–1½ oz (0.5–0.6 mm). The average leather trouser skin will be about 1¾–2 oz (0.7–0.8 mm). Leather outerwear is generally 2–2¼ oz (0.8–0.9 mm).

If you were planning the leather purchase for a long full skirt you would choose low-weight lambskin over pigskin. Yet, if you were making a pair of suede jeans, you might consider pig suede over lamb suede for its weight and durability.

SKIN SIZE

Skin sizes vary from animal to animal. The term **skin** applies to the pelt of a small animal. The pelt on a larger animal is referred to as a *hide*. Some skins, such as goatskin, can be as small as 2 sq ft (0.18 sq cm) per entire skin. Yet, a whole cowskin can be as large as 60 sq ft (5.5 sq m). In fact, because of the extremely large size of horse, cow and buffalo skins, most tanneries cut these skins in half, down the back, before shipping them to manufacturers. Manufacturers and tanneries refer to these half hides as **side leather**.

The size of a skin often defines how many **cuts (or cut lines)** you'll need in your design. These are the seams required to make your garment. Obviously, if you're planning to create a long suede coat in goatskin, you'll need more seams (or cuts) than if you were using larger skins. So, if you want to avoid cut lines in your garment you'd select a larger skin, such as pig, cow or even horse. However, because leather is expensive, you'll reduce the cost of the garment by increasing the number of cuts used in the garment. Think of the pattern pieces as puzzle pieces. The smaller they are, the easier they are to interlock, so all of the skin can be utilized. The larger the pattern pieces, the more difficult it will be to interlock them. This will result in a lot of wastage.

It is very important to make the cuts part of the design. There is nothing uglier than a garment with ill-placed cuts. Poorly-conceived cuts can ruin an otherwise beautiful garment. This will be discussed in more detail later (see page 88).

Previous spread: Good planning and selection of leathers was required to make this carefully crafted patchwork coat by Malandrino for the 2003 collection.

SKIN MEASURING

The standard system of measurement is by the square foot (0.092 sq m). Since the skins are not square but have an irregular shape, it is impossible for tanneries to measure a perfect square foot. Therefore, tanneries use a measuring machine (see Figure 4–1). They stamp two numbers on the backs of the skins. Usually, the first number is much larger than the second number so you can read them more easily. The first number is the full square footage. The second number is the remaining percentage of a square foot represented in quarters. For example '5 1' would be 5¼ sq ft (0.48 sq m), '5 2' is 5½ sq ft (0.51 sq m) and '5 3' is 5¾ sq ft (0.53 sq m).

When calculating the consumption of your design, you should estimate the average size of the skins you will be using, then use your pattern pieces to estimate how many skins you'll use to create each garment. For example, if the average size of an English domestic leather skin is 7 sq ft (0.65 sq m), draw an area on paper equivalent to this. This would usually be a rectangle approximately 2 x 3½ ft (0.60 x 1 m). Lay your pattern pieces on top of the 'skin'. Once you've covered the skin with as many pattern pieces as possible, set those pieces aside and lay the remaining pattern pieces on the skin. When you have used all of your pattern pieces, add up the total skin area you have used.

Remember that leather/suede skins are natural products – there may be scars, holes, wrinkles and other undesirable blemishes on the skin. To allow for these, you should add extra footage to your calculations. Add an additional allowance of 10 per cent if you plan to use low-quality skins. Add an additional allowance of 5 per cent if you plan to use high-quality skins.

If you want to translate one of your existing fabric designs to leather, you can calculate the leather footage required by using the formulas in Table 4–3.

TABLE 4–3 LEATHER FOOTAGE CONVERSIONS

FABRIC GARMENT		LEATHER GARMENT
WIDTH	LENGTH	LEATHER AREA
1.37 m (54 inches)	0.91 m (1 yd)	1.2 sq m (13 sq ft)
0.91 m (36 inches)	0.91 m (1 yd)	0.83 sq m (9 sq ft)

NOTE: Always add the 5–10 percent waste allowance to any fabric-to-leather translations.

Jean Claude Jitrois uses lambskin and fox for this coat, paired with stretched lambskin trousers for his 2008 collection.

Figure 4–1: A measuring machine.

SKIN CHARACTERISTICS

The following chart describes the key characteristics of different types of leather or suede.

TABLE 4–4 CHARACTERISTICS OF DIFFERENT TYPES OF LEATHER

SKIN TYPE	SKIN SIZE sq m (sq ft)	WEIGHT kg (oz)	CHARACTERISTICS
ANTELOPE	0.46–0.83 (5–9)	0.05–0.08 (2–3)	Very fine, lightweight, velvety nap; soft
BUCKSKIN	0.65–0.83 (7–9)	0.05–0.37 (2–4)	Originally made of buckskin or deerskin. Now made of calfskin or sheepskin; soft, strong and durable
CHAMOIS	0.65–0.83 (7–9)	0.18–0.27 (2–3)	Originally made from antelope skin; now made from the underside of sheep, lamb or calf. Tanned with fish oil or cod liver oil to make it stronger and more resilient; soft, light, small skins; pale-yellow in colour; washable
LAMB SUEDE	0.46–0.65 (5–7)	0.18–0.27 (2–3)	Made from young sheep or lamb. Soft, very fine, fluid and drapey
SHEEPSKIN	0.65–0.83 (7–9)	0.18–0.27 (2–3)	Similar texture and appearance to lambskin
SPLIT COWHIDE	1.67–2.32 (18–25)	0.18–0.09 (2 –3½)	Made when a thick cowskin is split into two thinner skins; characterized by being sueded on both sides; rough texture, strong
PIG SUEDE	0.83–1.48 (9–16)	0.27–0.37 (3–4)	The skin is characterized by groups of three tiny holes, caused by removal of the animal's hair; strong, durable and firm; less expensive than lamb suede, but more expensive than cow split
PIG SPLIT	0.83–1.48 (9–16)	0.27–0.37 (3–4)	Made when a thick pigskin is split into two thinner skins; characterized by being sueded on both sides; rough texture, strong, durable and firm
KIDSKIN	0.27–0.55 (3–6)	0.02–0.05 (1–2)	Made from a young goat; soft and pliable; not always sueded
GOAT SUEDE	0.37–0.55 (4–6)	0.05–0.08 (2–3)	From a mature goat; soft, but not as soft as lamb suede; skins are smaller than lamb and are more dense
CALFSKIN	0.83–1.39 (9–15)	0.04–0.11 (1½–4)	Made from the skin of young cows; close, fine smooth grain
CAPESKIN	0.27–0.83 (3–9)	0.04–0.08 (1½–3)	Made from South African hair or wool sheep; soft, but strong
CABRETTA	0.46–0.83 (5–9)	0.05–0.08 (2–3)	Spanish word meaning 'goat'; now made from a South American hair sheep rather than a wool-type sheep; smooth, pliant but tends to stretch
COWHIDE	1.67–2.32 (18–25)	0.34–0.38 (2–3½)	Strong, firm, durable and thick; not as smooth as calfskin; less expensive than lamb or calf
DOESKIN	0.27–0.46 (3–5)	0.02–0.05 (1–2)	Usually lambskin or sheepskin. Light, soft, supple, fine suede finish; washable
DEERSKIN	0.83 (9)	0.08–0.11 (3–4)	Made from elk and deer with the grain left intact; tanned in fish oil; soft, but strong; has a yellow-beige tint; washable

TABLE 4–4 (CONTINUED)

SKIN TYPE	SKIN SIZE sq m (sq ft)	WEIGHT kg (oz)	CHARACTERISTICS
HORSE	2.32–3.25 (25–35)	0.04–0.11 (1¼–4)	A rough-type skin, with lots of blemishes and irregular shading (unless pigmented); 'shell cordovan' comes from a horse's hind quarters; pony skins are 25 sq ft, horse skins are 35 (+) sq ft
PIGSKIN	0.83–1.48 (9–16)	0.08–0.11 (3–4)	Distinctive surface grain; tough, durable
OSTRICH	1.11–1.3 (12–14)	0.05–0.08 (2–3)	Bird skin known for the small bumps left on the skin once the feathers are removed; this effect is often seen on embossed leathers; comes from South Africa, Israel and Zimbabwe
PECCARY	0.83–1.48 (9–16)	0.08–0.11 (3–4)	Central and South American wild boar; looks like pigskin
HAIR SHEEP	0.37–0.55 (4–6)	0.01–0.02 (¼–1)	Sheep whose wool is hair-like
LAMBSKIN	0.46–0.65 (5–7)	0.01–0.02 (¼–1)	Skin from a lamb or young sheep
KIDSKIN	0.83–1.39 (9–15)	0.01–0.11 (1½–4)	Male or female bovine skin, sized between a calf and a mature animal
SHEARLING	0.46–0.65 (5–7)	0.02–0.05 (1–2)	Woolled lambskins and sheep with the wool intact
GOAT LEATHER	0.37–0.55 (4–6)	0.05–0.08 (2–3)	The grainy side has a raspy feel
VEALSKIN	0.83–1.39 (9–15)	0.04–0.11 (1½–4)	A large calfskin
ENGLISH DOMESTIC	0.46–0.65 (5–7)	0.01–0.02 (½–1)	Lambskin from England; a tight, clean-looking skin
NEW ZEALAND LAMB	0.46–0.65 (5–7)	0.01–0.02 (½–1)	Lambskin from New Zealand; grainy and easier to stretch than English domestic
COBRA	0.27–0.37 (3–4)	0.01 (½)	Large snake from Asia and Southeast Asia
LIZARD	0.09–0.13 (1–1½)	0.02 (1)	Has tiny scales; usually from South America and Indonesia
SHARK	0.13–0.65 (1½–7)	0.04–0.08 (1½–3)	Has small scales, usually brown or white or black and white; very durable; comes from the Caribbean and Gulf of Mexico; *Note:* Some species are endangered
ELEPHANT	8–10/PC.	0.05–0.22 (2–8)	Very thick, tough skins, usually grey or brown; uneven skin; *Note:* Some species are endangered
HIPPOPOTAMUS	See size note–>	0.05–0.22 (2–8)	Large, unique grain; *Size note:* sold in sections of various sizes; *Note:* Endangered
ANACONDA	0.55–0.83 (6–9)	0.04 (1½)	South American; *Note:* Some species are endangered

TABLE 4–5 NOVELTY SKINS

TYPE	CHARACTERISTICS
PATENT LEATHER	Any leather treated with a waterproof film on one surface. The treated surface is lustrous and reflective.
PEARLIZED LEATHER	Any leather that has been given a coloured, pearl-like lustre.
EMBOSSED LEATHER	Any leather that has a motif in relief. The embossing is achieved with a metal template, heat and pressure.
PRINTED LEATHER/ SUEDE	Skins that have been silk screened or painted.
DISTRESSED LEATHER	Skins that have been treated to look worn and rough. Manufacturers achieve this either by a mechanical process or by screen printing.
NU-BUCK	A skin whose grain side has been buffed. Often used on lamb, cow or calf. The resulting skin looks like suede, but with a tight, low pile.

TABLE 4–6 SPECIALITY SKINS

TYPE	SKIN SIZE sq m (sq ft)	WEIGHT kg (oz)	CHARACTERISTICS
ALLIGATOR	0.55–1.3 (6–14)	N/A	Similar to crocodile but less pronounced and shorter snout. Some species are endangered.
PYTHON	0.74–1.8 (8–20)	N/A	A large snakeskin – up to 76 cm (30 inches) long – used mostly for bags, shoes and boots.
FROG	0.37–0.55 (4–6)	N/A	Small skins from Japan. Usually made into wallets. Some species are endangered.
SEAL	DO NOT USE	N/A	Black shiny leather. Endangered.
FISH	0.09–0.18 (1–2)	N/A	Usually salmon, carp or cod.
WHIP SNAKE	0.55 (6)	N/A	Indian water snakes. Fairly inexpensive. Excellent for trims
CROCODILE	0.15–0.40 (1½–4)	N/A	Stiff with a scale texture. Some species are endangered.

NOTE: Speciality skins are not usually sold by weight. When you buy these, you can expect relatively consistent weights from skin to skin.

PURCHASING SKIN

You should almost always purchase skins in person. This may sometimes involve travelling to faraway places, at great expense. However, if you are purchasing large quantities of skins, you could actually save money by improving the overall quality and yield of your purchase. When you're inspecting skins, here is what you should look out for:

· Be certain that you are really being shown the skin you requested. Sometimes, a dealer will try to pass off one skin as another. Unless you are knowledgeable about the skin you are looking for, you may be tricked.
· Study the characteristics chart in this book (see Table 4–4) and make sure you know what a particular skin should look like.
· Smell the skin. Does it have an obnoxious odour? Some improperly tanned skins have a bad odour that cannot be eliminated by dry cleaning.

NAMES OF PARTS OF A LEATHER SKIN

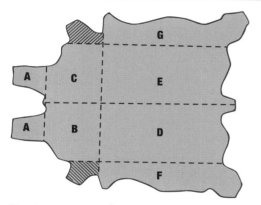

Head	A
Shoulder	B+C
Bend	D or E
Belly	F or G
Side	A+B+D+F or A+C+E+G
Back	B+D or C+E

When examining a skin, remember that the nappa, or outside, should be the best quality part of the skin. If the nappa has excessive scars, holes or discolorations, then you know that you are not looking at a very good skin. You should expect to find weak spots, stretched areas, and stains or shading in the belly, neck and leg areas. Yet, despite these imperfections, clever cutters often make good use of these sections by including them in the hidden parts of a garment or in decorated accessories.

Watch out for tiny holes in the skin. You may not be able to see these holes if you view the skin flat on a table, so you will need to hold it up to the light. Small holes become larger over time and can ruin your finished garments.

Uneven dyeing causes **shading**. Shading exists when different parts of a skin show colour variations and it makes it impossible to match different sections of a garment when sewing it together. You will have to accept minor shading differences in full aniline skins. You will also have shading problems with semi-aniline skins, although you may have slightly fewer than with aniline skins, due to their special spray processing.

Choose skins with roughly the same weight. Skins often vary within the same bundle. You would not want one sleeve to be thicker than the other.

Make sure that the grain or surface of your skins have continuity. Some skins are grainier than others. Fine garments should boast uniform grain.

You should also match the colours on all of your skins. Since there may be different shades of the same colour in one bundle, you should always lay the skins out by folding them in half and placing them on top of each other with about 15 cm (6 inches) of each skin showing. This will enable you to view all of the skins at a glance.

As discussed earlier, you should calculate how many skins will be needed for your design and purchase more than that number. Skins that have many blemishes will produce poor yield, so you should always buy more skins than you need – if you run short, it may not be possible to obtain replacement skins in the proper shade.

If you order skins by mail or phone, make sure that you clearly communicate the type and quality of skins you require. If the supplier doesn't have the skins you need and offers you a substitute, ask for a sample of the skin for approval before placing your order. Always specify which skin size you want. If you plan on cutting 6-sq ft (0.55-sq m) skins and they send you 4-sq ft (0.37-sq m) skins, you might not have enough raw skins to complete your production run.

Generally, skins are purchased according to a percentage breakdown of A, B or C quality skins. Some suppliers refer to them as 1st, 2nd or 3rd quality skins. You might even see them described as Type #1, Type #2 etc. A typical selection might be either: 60% A, 30% B, 10% C, or 50% A, 30% B, 20% C. However, the percentage breakdown will vary from tannery to tannery.

A **bundle** is defined as a 12-skin unit. Bundles usually come rolled and tied. A **pack** usually represents about 3,000 sq ft (278 sq m) of leather. Tanneries ship packs in large boxes containing bundles. If you are buying a small quantity, such as 40 sq ft (3.7 sq m), a dealer may not want to break open a whole bundle for you and may ask you to purchase the whole bundle.

If you only want to buy A or 1st quality skins, most suppliers will want to charge you a price premium of +30%, unless you're a very good, long-term customer, or are purchasing huge quantities. Some dealers may not sell you small quantities of exclusively A skins at all.

PLANNING YOUR DESIGN

Whether you are working with your own pattern or a commercial pattern from one of the major pattern companies, such as Simplicity or McCall's, you will need to note the following:

1. Think before you start making your patterns and, especially, before you purchase your skins. Think about your end user, the person who will eventually buy your garment.

2. If you plan to use very thin skins, remember that your purchaser will find it very easy to scuff or scrape such skins, increasing the probability of returns. A heavier skin, although not as fashionable, will wear much better over time.

3. Will your purchaser be able to clean your garment, without risk?

· Avoid combining highly contrasting colours, for example black with white, unless you have confirmed that the darker colour's dyes won't run into the lighter-coloured sections when the garment is dry cleaned. Use the **white handkerchief test** to confirm the stability of a garment's colour. Rub the handkerchief along the inner facing of the garment. If the colour comes off easily, you will have colour bleeding problems.

· Don't attach hardware to your garment, unless you believe a dry cleaner could easily remove it before cleaning.

4. Have you properly matched your choice of skin to the type of garment you plan to design? For example, if you are designing a coat, don't select lamb suede as it is too delicate and would not wear as well as lamb leather. You might use a 0.4–0.5 mm (1–1¼ oz) pig suede for a shirt, but not for a fitted skirt. You might use a 0.7–0.8 mm (1¾ –2 oz) pig suede for a skirt, but not for a shirt.

5. Always make a muslin of your garment, whether you plan to use the flat pattern method, the draping method or a commercial pattern. By making a muslin first, you can always make any necessary adjustments to the muslin *before* you cut the skins.

Once the pattern has been cut, it will not be easy to make adjustments. You do not want to repair a garment after it has been sewn, as the re-sewn garment will show some of its old holes.

Suede is a little more forgiving. The holes created when sewing a suede garment are relatively small. However, you can avoid the need to repair your brand new garment by creating a **fitting muslin** before cutting. This fitting muslin will enable you to confirm the appropriateness of the placement of the cuts in your garment, if they are required, for that type of leather.

Using styling tape, place your cut lines (see Figures 4–2 and 4–3). Place them where they will be the least noticeable, unless you are using them as design details.

Make sure you make enough cuts to make the most of the size of your skins. Always ask yourself if any of your pattern pieces will be bigger than the average high quality portion of your skins.

You should try to avoid placing cut lines at stress points in your garment. For example, do not place a cut line on the knee area of a pair of trousers. Always place it above or below the knee. There

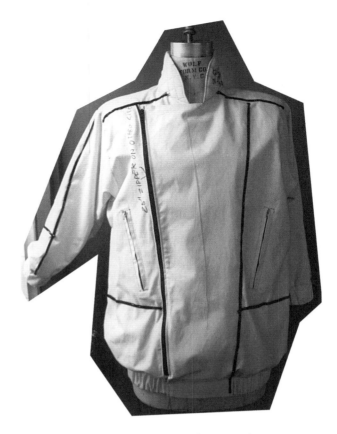

Figure 4–2: Front of a muslin using styling tape to denote cuts.

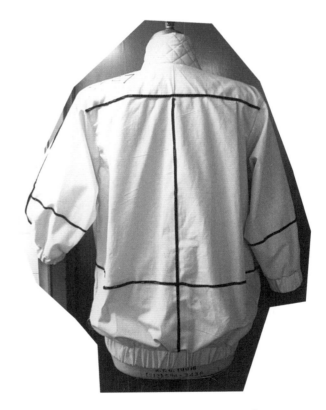

Figure 4–3: Back of a muslin showing styling tape to denote cuts.

are also some aesthetic considerations. For example, cut lines at the hip and thigh level on a skirt or trousers tend to make women look wider in that area.

The more cut lines you add to your garment, the less skin you will use. This is because you will be able to fit more tightly interlocked pieces from each single skin, like a jigsaw puzzle (see Figure 4–4).

By adding a cut line to the same design, dividing the front and back leg of the shorts, we can get even more pattern pieces from the same skin (see Figure 4–5). Once you have decided where to place the cut lines you will make a hard pattern.

In a typical leather garment factory, where several hundred garments might be cut from one pattern, a hard cardboard template is made from the original pattern. The factory uses an electric cardboard pattern cutter, a special electric saw, such as the Stanley Industrial Unishear, to create these durable pattern pieces (see Figure 4–6).

Even if you wish to cut smaller quantities of skin, you should make (and use) **oak-tag patterns**. Hard patterns provide you with better cutting stability, allowing you to cut sharp clean edges. Always make a hard copy of a commercial pattern. The paper on which commercial patterns are printed is essentially tissue paper. If you don't copy to hard pattern it will deteriorate quickly.

To make a hard pattern, get a piece of oak tag or any other thick, firm paper. Fold the paper so that you have a double layer of paper. Staple the free edges together, then cut the doubled-over paper into the proper pattern shape (see Figure 4–7).

Seam allowances should be about 8–10 mm (⅜–½ inch) for most seams. However, you should provide a 5-mm (¼-inch) seam allowance for seams that are stitched and turned, for example collar edges and pocket flaps.

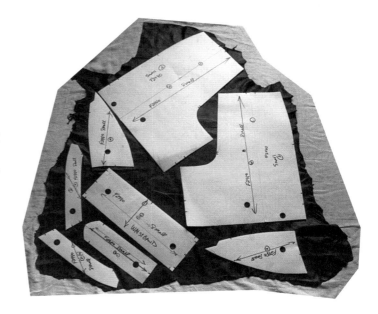

Figure 4–4: This pair of shorts shows poor utilization of skin.

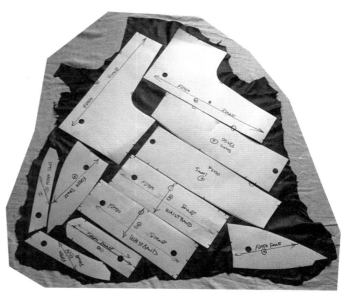

Figure 4–5: This pair of shorts shows better utilization of skin.

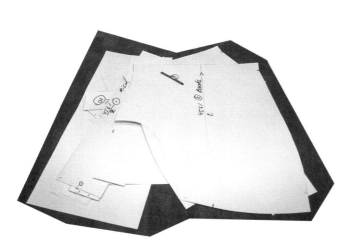

Figure 4–7: An oak-tag pattern.

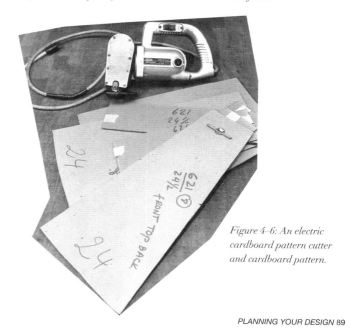

Figure 4–6: An electric cardboard pattern cutter and cardboard pattern.

CHAPTER 5
CREATING A
DESIGN/SPEC
SHEET

Garment manufacture today is a truly international industry. Clothes may be designed in one country and manufactured in another. Key to this process is the design/spec sheet on which all the information needed to make the garment is written. In this chapter we will learn how to create and fill in a spec sheet to ensure the finished garment matches the original design.

USING A DESIGN/ SPEC SHEET

Once the garment is designed, some companies will make a prototype and send it to the manufacturer – whether that manufacturer is located in the same country or elsewhere – while others may send only a design/spec sheet.

The factory will make the first prototype by reading the design/ spec sheet and following its instructions. The sheet lists many specifications. The more measurements that you can give the person making the pattern in your manufacturing facility, the more accurate your first sample will be.

The process follows these stages:
1. The designer either faxes, emails, mails or hand delivers the design/spec sheet to the pattern maker at the factory.
2. The pattern maker makes a pattern and the first sample or prototype from the design/spec sheet.
3. The designer then examines the first sample for construction, size specifications and overall 'look'.
4. The designer notes any corrections directly on the design/spec sheet under the category 'second prototype' and returns it to the pattern maker at the factory.
5. The pattern maker makes further corrections to the original prototype, or creates a new one, then sends the second prototype to the designer.
6. If necessary, the process may continue to a third or fourth prototype. However, the style is usually fully corrected by the second prototype.
7. The factory then makes a final production sample for reference.

In the following pages, you will see a design/spec sheet for a basic shirt. This form can also be used to define the specs of a jacket and/or a coat. Following the example of a shirt, you will see how the same form can be used to spec out a jacket.

Previous spread: The unusual design of this leather jacket and shorts with integrated back pocket by Bonnie Cashin in 1974 means that the design/spec sheet would have been created with particular care.

Jordan Betten of Lost Art creates rock star chic with snakeskin trousers and tan leather jacket for musician Lenny Kravitz.

COMPANY:	DESIGN INSTINCT	STYLE NO:	5039
SKIN:	LAMB SUEDE	DATE:	06/12/09
GARMENT DESCRIPTION:	WOMEN'S BASIC SHIRT	LABEL:	DESIGN INSTINCT
COUNTRY OF ORIGIN:	KOREA	HANGTAG:	DESIGN INSTINCT

SHELL		CONTRAST A		CONTRAST B		CONTRAST C	
COLOUR:	RED	COLOUR:		COLOUR:		COLOUR:	

LINING	INTERLINING	INTERFACING	POCKETING
BODY (UPPER): RAYON/ACETATE	BODY:		
BODY (LOWER):			
SLEEVES NONE	SLEEVES	TRICOT	
TRIM			

BUTTON	NO. 2199 L/24-7	KNIT:	
POPPER:		VELCRO:	
ZIP:		FUR TRIM:	
PULL:		ELASTIC:	
DRAWSTRING:		BUCKLE:	
EYELET:		SHOULDER PAD:	
STOPPER:		CONTRAST TOPSTICH:	

SKETCH:

SIZE SPECIFICATION	PROTOTYPE CM (INCHES)	2ND PROTOTYPE	PRODUCTION SAMPLE
SIZE: MEDIUM			
DATE: 05/12/09			
Body length @ centre back:	73.6 (29)		
Centre back waist length:			
Across back shoulder	53.3 (21)		
Across back shoulder 12.7 cm (5 inches) down CB	48.2 (19)		
Shoulder slope	19.6 (7¾)		
Waist extended ½	59.6 (23½)		
Waist relaxed ½			
Bottom width ½	58.4 (23)		
Depth of armhole			
Armhole front curve	25 (10)		
Armhole back curve	26 (10¼)		
Sleeve length from shoulder	74.9 (29½)		
Sleeve length from CB	82.5 (32½)		
Sleeve muscle 2.5 cm (1 inch) down armhole ½	22.2 (8¾)		
Sleeve 5 cm (2 inches) above edge/cuff ½	15.8 (6¼)		
Sleeve opening ½	15.2 (6)		
Cuff height			
Across front raglan 25 cm (10 inches) down from HPS			
Across back raglan 25 cm (10 inches) down from HPS			
Armhole front raglan			
Armhole back raglan			
Bust/chest ½ 2.5 cm (1 inch) down armhole	58.4 (23)		
Neck opening inside	12.7 (5)		
Neckline from notch to notch			

DESIGN/SPEC SHEET SHIRT/JACKET/COAT (PART 3)

SIZE SPECIFICATION	PROTOTYPE CM (INCHES)	2ND PROTOTYPE SAMPLE	PRODUCTION
SIZE: MEDIUM			
DATE: 05/12/09			
Front neck drop (HPS)	6.3 (2½)		
Back neck drop (HPS)	1.2 (½)		
Collar height at CB	6.3 (2½)		
Collar stand	3.1 (1¼)		
Collar height at CF			
Collar point	7.9 (3⅛)		
Lapel point			
Placket width			
Placket length			
Yoke height front (HPS)			
Yoke height back (HPS)			
Chest pocket from HPS			
Chest pocket from CF	23.4 (9¼)		
Body pocket from HPS	8.9 (3½)		
Body Pocket from CF			
Upper pocket flap width/length			
Upper pocket width/length			
Lower pocket width/length			
Lower pocket flap width/length			
Pocket welt width/length			

COMMENTS/SPECIAL INSTRUCTIONS:

SELF-COLOUR EDGESTITCH AROUND COLLAR AND CENTRE FRONT, SHIRT TAIL BOTTOM, COLLAR STAND AND POCKET. TOPSTITCH SLEEVE HEM 2.5 CM (1 INCH) FROM EDGE.

The following design/spec sheet is for a drawstring jacket. You'll notice that the form is the same as that used for the shirt.

DESIGN/SPEC SHEET · SHIRT/JACKET/COAT (PART 1)

COMPANY:	DESIGN INSTINCT	STYLE NO:	3066
SKIN:	LAMB LEATHER	DATE:	09/03/09
GARMENT DESCRIPTION:	MEN'S DRAWSTRING JACKET	LABEL:	DESIGN INSTINCT
COUNTRY OF ORIGIN:	INDIA	HANGTAG:	DESIGN INSTINCT

SHELL		CONTRAST A		CONTRAST B		CONTRAST C
COLOUR:	BLACK	COLOUR:		COLOUR:		COLOUR:

LINING	INTERLINING	INTERFACING	POCKETING
BODY (UPPER): FLANEL BODY (LOWER): TWILL ACETATE	BODY: THINSULATE	TRICOT	TWILL ACETATE
SLEEVES TWILL ACETATE TRIM NO.2 TAPE	SLEEVES THINSULATE		

BUTTON		KNIT:	
POPPER:	NO. 6199 1/3-9 TOTAL	VELCRO:	
ZIP:	63.5 CM (25 INCH) DTM PLASTIC NO. 5	FUR TRIM:	
PULL:	NO. 209 DTM	ELASTIC:	
DRAWSTRING:	NO. 29 DTM	BUCKLE:	
EYELET:		SHOULDER PAD:	
STOPPER:		CONTRAST TOPSTICH:	

SKETCH:

DESIGN/SPEC SHEET | SHIRT/JACKET/COAT (PART 2)

SIZE SPECIFICATION	PROTOTYPE CM (INCHES)	2ND PROTOTYPE	PRODUCTION SAMPLE
SIZE: MEDIUM			
DATE: 10/10/09			
Body length @ centre back:	86 (34)		
Centre back waist length:	50.8 (20)		
Across back shoulder			
Across back shoulder 12.7 cm (5 inches) down CB			
Shoulder slope			
Waist extended ½	64.7 (25½)		
Waist relaxed ½			
Bottom width ½	64.7 (25½)		
Depth of armhole			
Armhole front curve			
Armhole back curve			
Sleeve length from shoulder	81.9 (32¼)		
Sleeve length from CB	93.9 (37)		
Sleeve muscle 2.5 cm (1 inch) down armhole ½	30.4 (12)		
Sleeve 5 cm (2 inch) above edge/cuff ½	18.4 (7¼)		
Sleeve opening ½	10.8 (4¼)		
Cuff height	5.7 (2¼)		
Across front raglan 25 cm (10 inches) down from HPS	55.8 (22)		
Across back raglan 25 cm (10 inches) down from HPS	56.5 (22½)		
Armhole front raglan	41.9 (16½)		
Armhole back raglan	50.1 (19¾)		
Bust/chest ½ 2.5 cm (1 inch) down armhole	68.5 (27)		
Neck opening inside	15.2 (6)		
Neckline from notch to notch			
Front neck drop (HPS)	13.3 (5¼)		
Back neck drop (HPS)	1.2 (½)		

DESIGN/SPEC SHEET | SHIRT/JACKET/COAT (PART 3)

SIZE SPECIFICATION	PROTOTYPE CM (INCHES)	2ND PROTOTYPE	PRODUCTION SAMPLE
SIZE: MEDIUM			
DATE: 10/10/09			
Collar height at CB	10.1 (4)		
Collar stand			
Collar height at CG			
Collar point	9.5 (3¾)		
Lapel point			
Placket width	6.9 (2⅜)		
Placket length	73 (28¾)		
Yoke height front (HPS)			
Yoke height back (HPS)			
Chest pocket from HPS	29.2 (11½)		
Chest pocket from CF	19 (7½)		
Body pocket from HPS	57.7 (22¾)		
Body pocket from CF	6.9 (2⅜)		
Upper pocket flap width/length	6.3 X 17.8 (2½ X 7)		
Upper pocket width/length			
Lower pocket width/length			
Lower pocket flap width/length	20.3 X 7.6 (8 X 3)		
Pocket welt width/length	1.9 X 15.2 (¾ X 6)		

COMMENTS/SPECIAL INSTRUCTIONS:

SELF-COLOUR DOUBLE NEEDLE TOPSTITCH: COLLAR, PLACKET, POCKET FLAPS, CUFFS, SHOULDER SEAM, CENTRE BACK SEAM. DECORATIVE ZIGZAG STITCH ON FRONT PLACKET AND COLLAR, WIDTH OF PLACKET 10.4 CM (4⅛ INCHES) APART. EDGESTITCH WAIST SEAM AND AROUND WELT POCKET. OPEN SEAMS ON SLEEVES. TOPSTITCH 1.9 CM (¾ INCH) UP FROM HEM ON SLEEVES.

The following design/spec sheet is for a pair of trousers or a skirt, showing specifically how such a form might be filled out for a pair of pleated trousers.

DESIGN/SPEC SHEET · TROUSERS/SKIRT (PART 1)

COMPANY:	DESIGN INSTINCT	STYLE NO:	3221
SKIN:	LAMB LEATHER	DATE:	18/10/09
GARMENT DESCRIPTION:	WOMEN'S PLEATED TROUSERS	LABEL:	DESIGN INSTINCT
COUNTRY OF ORIGIN:	CHINA	HANGTAG:	DESIGN INSTINCT

SHELL		CONTRAST A		CONTRAST B		CONTRAST C
COLOUR:	BROWN	COLOUR:		COLOUR:		COLOUR:

LINING BODY	BODY INTERLINING	POCKETING	INTERFACING
RAYON / ACETATE			TRICOT

BUTTON	NO. 5641 DTM-1 TOTAL	KNIT:	
POPPER:		VELCRO:	
ZIP:	2.5–20.3 CM (1-8 INCHES) DTM	ELASTIC:	
PULL:		BUCKLE:	
DRAWSTRING:		CONTRAST TOPSTICH:	
EYELET:		STOPPER:	

SKETCH:

SIZE SPECIFICATION	PROTOTYPE CM (INCHES)	2ND PROTOTYPE	PRODUCTION SAMPLE
SIZE: MEDIUM			
DATE: 07/11/09			
Waist	71 (28)		
Front rise below waistband	30.4 (28)		
Back rise below waistband	35.5 (14)		
Thigh 2.5 cm (1 inch) below crotch seam ½	33 (13)		
Knee 30.4 (12 inches) below crotch seam ½	25.4 (10)		
Leg opening ½	17.7 (7)		
Inseam length	78.7 (31)		
Outseam length	107.9 (42½)		
Belt loop width/length	0.95 (⅜) X 4.4 (1¾)		
Waistband width ½	3.1 (1¼)		
Waistband length edge to edge ½	38.1 (15)		
High hip 10 cm (4 inches) below waistband ½	47 (18½)		
Hip at 17.7 cm (7 inches) below WBN ½	6.3 (2½)		
Skirt length below WBN			
Sweep ½			
Pocket width	1.2 (½)		
Pocket length	14.28 (5⅝)		

COMMENTS/SPECIAL INSTRUCTIONS:

SELF-COLOUR EDGESTITCH: AROUND POCKET WELT, WAISTBAND LOOP EDGES AND
FLY FRONT. BOUND BUTTONHOLE ON WAISTBAND. TROUSERS ARE FULLY LINED.

CHAPTER 6
SORTING, SHADING
AND CUTTING

There are two key considerations in making a leather garment, the first of which is to choose your skins carefully, ensuring they match, in a process known as sorting and shading. The second is the cutting of leather, which is a specialized technique, different to that used for any other material. This chapter will discuss these unique stages of leather garment manufacture.

SORTING AND SHADING

The colour and grain of leather can vary significantly from one skin to another. To achieve a good overall appearance in your finished garment, you must first sort and shade the skins so that all the pieces look the same. If your design requires 40 sq ft (3.71 sq m) of leather, select 48–50 sq ft (4.45–4.64 sq m) and check consistency (see Figure 6–1).

CUTTING

While manufacturers of fabric garments usually ply several layers of fabric on top of one another before cutting, the manufacturers of leather and suede garments always cut one skin at a time. Because leather skins vary greatly in size and quality, manufacturers always cut skins individually, placing a pattern piece on top of each skin. You should do the same yourself. Never try to cut two pieces at a time by folding a skin in half.

Leather garment manufacturers cut leathers on a special wooden leather cutting board (see Figure 6–2). They use a **short knife**, sharpened on a special sharpening stone, to cut the skins (see Figure 6–3). Leather cutters like to use a short knife because it is small and fits nicely into the palm. It also has replaceable blades to facilitate the replacement of dull blades.

A professional leather cutter would place each pattern piece on the 'right side', the nappa or outside of the skin, avoiding any flaws. He holds the pattern down with one hand while he cuts the skin, using the short knife, with his other hand (see Figure 6–4). He may also use a weight to hold down the pattern. He would then use an awl to poke small holes for darts. He would use the short knife to make the short cuts for notches.

The **marking and scissor method** is an alternative to the short knife method. Working with the same hard paper pattern, you place the pattern on the 'right side' of the skin. Place a weight on the pattern to keep it stable (see Figure 6–5). Trace around the pattern piece with a pencil or fine tipped, waterproof marking pen, marking all the notches (see Figure 6–6). *Do not use an ink pen* as it may smudge. You may use an awl to mark the darts by puncturing small holes, but *do not* mark the darts with a pen since, when sewing, it is easier to see the markings on the 'wrong side'.

Once all the parts have been marked, you may cut, using sharp dressmaking shears, either 17- or 25-cm (7- or 10-inch) lengths. You should cut on the inside of your marking line since, if you do not, you might add extra width and length. Make certain that none of your notches is deeper than 6 mm (¼ inch). If they are cut deeper than this, the notches may eventually cause the leather or suede to tear or split in that area. Once you have cut all of the pieces, matching right sides together in pairs, roll them up and tie them together. This will keep the skins from creasing until you are ready to sew them (see Figure 6–7).

Previous spread: Dyed leathers for this patchwork coat by Zang Toi from 1992 would have been carefully sorted to ensure consistency of colour and grain.

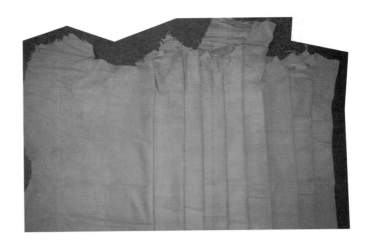

Figure 6–1: How to confirm colour consistency.

Figure 6–2: A leather cutting board.

Figure 6–3: A short knife and a sharpening stone.

Figure 6–4: Cutting with a short knife.

STORING SKINS

You should never fold unused leather or suede. If you do, the creases along fold lines may not come out. If possible, you should store the skins flat or draped over a padded surface. If this is impossible, then they can be loosely rolled. Place the nappa side of two skins face to face, then roll them up together. Don't store them near heat or in range of the sun, as they might dry out and fade. Overly dried out skins can become brittle and tear easily.

Figure 6–5: Using a weight to hold down a pattern while cutting.

CUTTING TIPS

Since the yield of each piece of leather is often too small to allow you to cut both the left and right sides of the front of a blouse or jacket from the same skin, you will often find yourself cutting several different, and often unrelated, pattern pieces from the same skin. When you do this, make sure you don't forget what sides of the garment you've already cut. To help you remember where you are in a cutting job, flip over each left/right pattern piece as soon as you've cut from it, and set it aside. Make sure that you set the already used pattern piece with the still-to-be-cut side facing up. When you've cut as much as you can from one skin, you can use the pattern pieces you've set aside to cut from the next skin. Having set aside the once used pattern pieces facing up on their still-to-be-cut sides, you won't forget which sides you've already cut and which sides are yet to be cut.

Figure 6–6: Marking with a pencil.

As you cut each pattern piece, keep in mind which sits next to which in the garment. This will allow you to match grains and colours that much better. Also note that the stretchy areas of the skin should not be placed at the stress points of the garment or anywhere very visible. The vertical dimensions of the main sections of the garment should be cut from the lengthways dimension of the skin. This makes sure that the left-to-right dimension of your garment enjoys the stretchier, crossways grain of the animal.

The smaller pieces can be laid either crossways or lengthways on the skin to produce the best skin yield. If you are cutting a printed or embossed skin, then you must cut it so that the design on each piece goes in the same direction. Some suedes, such as pig suede, boast a very definite nap 'design'. If you have such a suede, cut all of the pattern pieces in the same direction.

Figure 6–7: Some cut pattern pieces rolled up for storage.

Never stretch a skin to produce a bigger yield. If you do, the pieces will shrink back and will not fit together easily. The result will be an ill-fitting and poorly shaped garment.

CHAPTER 7
PUTTING YOUR
LEATHER GARMENT
TOGETHER

Leather is a much tougher material to handle than fabric and sewing leather consequently requires the use a number of specialist machines and pieces of equipment. In this chapter we will look at the tools for sewing leather, including sewing machines, needles and glue, which can be used to turn hems and make seams lie flat.

STITCHING

You can sew your leather garment by hand or using a machine, but you must use the correct equipment if you are to achieve a good result.

Make sure that you use a sewing machine that can handle the thickness and weight of your skins. Most home sewing machines will not be able to handle the weight of most leathers. Professional sewing machines use a three-cord thread, which is stronger than the usual cotton thread used to sew fabrics.

You should use an industrial machine, such as the Juki LU 2220N–7 (see Figure 7–1) which has a walking foot (see Figure 7–2), or a Juki DDL 8700L bottom-feed lockstitch machine, both of which can handle topstitching and sewing over several thicknesses of leather or suede.

Another option is the Brother Nouvelle PQ 1500S machine, a home sewing model with a walking foot attachment that is good for sewing medium thickness leathers or for closing seams (see Figure 7–3).

If you use an industrial straight stitch machine, then you should attach Teflon® teeth, foot and plate to your machine (see Figure 7–4). The stitch size should be no larger than 8–10 stitches per 2.5 cm (1 inch). Smaller stitches will result in tearing at the stitching line. The proper needle for the machine is a tripoint or diamond point size 16 or 18.

If you want to sew by hand, use a glover's needle. These range in size from 2 to 8. Size 2 is perfect for hand sewing buttons, trims or other details.

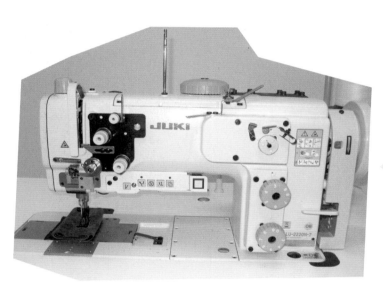

Figure 7–1: A Juki LU 2220N–7 walking foot machine.

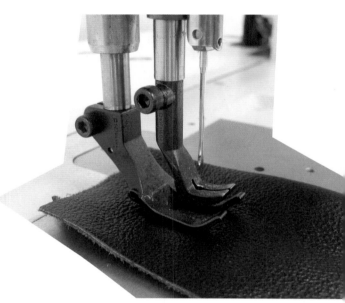

Figure 7–2: A needle bar on a walking foot machine.

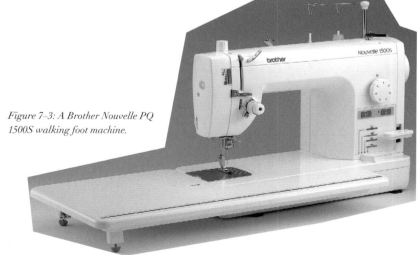

Figure 7–3: A Brother Nouvelle PQ 1500S walking foot machine.

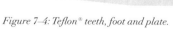

Figure 7–4: Teflon® teeth, foot and plate.

Previous spread: Thierry Mugler's black leather bustier and skirt from 1994 required stitching and hand lacing of seams and the application of metal studs and spikes.

GLUING

Gluing makes seams lie flat and eliminates excess bulk. Glue is also used to drape and fold the skin for certain effects. This can create a beautiful, highly styled garment.

In order to apply glue to a seam, you should use a brush and a roller tool (see Figure 7–5). The glue that is used in leather factories is a white cement available at professional supply companies under a number of brand names, for example Sobo®, Barge® cement and Magnatac 809. Some factories will use an oil can to apply the glue (see Figure 7–6).

However, you need to think about how dry cleaning will affect these glues. Most leather cleaners can replace glue in accessible areas of the garment, such as hems and seams. However, they may not be able to replace the glue in draped areas. If possible, try to make sure that you design around this problem by machine- or handstitching these hidden areas.

PRESSING

Leather or suede should never come in direct contact with an iron. Always place heavy brown paper between the iron and the garment you want to press.

Avoid steam and do not use a pressing or muslin cloth. Use a medium to low setting on the iron and press the garment evenly. Do not let the iron sit in one spot since this can create a permanent mark on the skin.

Figure 7–5: Some glue, a roller tool, a brush, a hammer and some cold tape.

Figure 7–6: An oil can, used to apply glue.

CHAPTER 8
LININGS AND
REINFORCEMENTS

*In the last chapter we looked at
some of the specialized equipment
needed to sew leather. Here we look
at some of the key sewing techniques
required to ensure a good finish to
garments, including the use of linings,
interlinings and seam reinforcement.*

LININGS

Jackets, in particular, require lining and reinforcment to ensure that the leather will not stretch across key seams, such as the shoulder seam. Lining also makes garments comfortable to wear.

Making a lining pattern for a leather garment is like making a lining for a cloth garment. Leather garments are lined more often than cloth garments since many people do not like the feel of animal skin next to their own skin. However, many designers will add only a half lining to shirts, lining the upper portion of the shirt.

Some skins, such as lamb suede, feel rough or look unsightly on the inside, so designers will usually add a lining to cover up the imperfections. If you want to make an unlined leather garment, purchase specially processed leathers whose insides are as attractive as their outsides.

Once you have made a fitting muslin, you should decide whether you want to back certain parts of your garment with lining. For example, you may want to consider using a lining fabric for the undersides of the pocket flaps, epaulettes, cuffs, collars or hoods. You may also want to use lining fabric to line certain hidden sections of the garment, for example the underlay of a wrap skirt or the underneath top yoke of a trench coat. This will not only save skins (and money), but it will also make the garment lighter.

UNDERLININGS

Based on the weight of your skins, you can add extra firmness to certain areas of your garment by underlining it. For example, you could use a **tricot fusible interfacing** to give a lamb suede blazer a more tailored look. Designers prefer tricot (rather than non-woven and woven fusible) as an underlining because it is knitted, allowing it to stretch when the garment is worn.

INTERLININGS AND FILLERS

Interlinings are materials that are applied underneath garment linings, usually for additional warmth. Many manufacturers seek to add these to their leather outerwear by either fully or partially insulating their garments. These materials are known as fillers – the two most popular product lines are made by 3M and DuPont.

Fillers are chosen based on their hand, feel and the desired appearance of the garment. Some fillers are designed to provide a very thin layer of material solely for insulation. Other fillers are designed to provide garments with a lofty, down-like look.

DUPONT PRODUCTS

These range in weight from 100–200 g (3½–7 oz) and are made of Dacron® polyester fibres.

THIN INSULATION
Thermolite®
Microloft®

MID-LOFT INSULATION
Thermoloft®

HIGH-LOFT INSULATION

Microloftallofil®
Quallofil®
Hallofil®
Hallofil II®

3M'S PRODUCTS

These are blends of polyolefin and polyester, ranging in weight from 40–250 g (1⅔–8⅔ oz) and include:

THIN INSULATION
Thinsulate®
Thinsulate Lite Loft®

MID-LOFT INSULATION
Thinsulate Ultra®

HIGH-LOFT INSULATION
Thinsulate Lite Loft®

INTERFACING

Designers apply interfacing to all seams that are sewn together and turned, such as pocket flaps, welt pockets, pocket tops, collars, lapels, waistbands, cuffs and the centre fronts of garments. Interfacing is also used to secure areas of stress in a garment such as around armholes, necklines, zips, pocket openings, buttonholes, buttons, hems and loops.

Several types of interfacing can be used. The most preferred interfacing is **fusible interfacing**, which is available in three types, non-woven fusible (see Figure 8–1), woven fusible and fusible tricot. In order to choose the correct interfacing, you should consider the type of skin you're using and the design of the garment. For example, if you're designing a soft lightweight lamb suede collar, you will need a soft interfacing and should consider using a lightweight woven fusible or a tricot.

Some pre-made fusible interfacings come by the roll for use in certain areas in the garment. These easy-to-use interfacings are perfect for the fronts of blouses, waistbands or cuffs. Some interfacings come with perforated guidelines, making them easy for the operator to sew.

Some factories order their own, custom-made, non-woven fusible interfacing in various widths for areas that need particular reinforcing, such as the zip area (see Figure 8–2).

Previous spread: Not only famous for the Birkin and Grace Kelly bag, Hermès creates some of the most sensational ready-to-wear leather, such as this tan leather jacket, teamed here with a sheer black skirt in 2007.

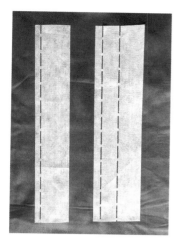

Figure 8–1: Non-woven, fusible interfacing with perforated guidelines.

Figure 8–2: Custom-made non-woven fusible interfacing.

SEAM REINFORCEMENTS

In addition to interfacing, you should consider using **cold tape** to further reinforce your seams and to prevent stretching, especially when you plan to topstitch the seams. Cold tape comes in three different widths: 6 mm (¼ inch), 9.5 mm (⅜ inch) and 25 mm (1 inch) (see Figure 8–3). The most commonly used is 9.5 mm (⅜ inch).

Cold tape has a sticky back. You apply it before sewing the seams together. You can use it on front openings, waistbands, zips, cuffs, pocket openings, pocket flaps, collars or anywhere that a garment needs extra support.

Although we will be discussing the use of cold tape further in later chapters, some applications for it are on the edge of a waistband (see Figure 8–4), on the stitching line of a zip (see Figure 8–5) and on the edge of a cuff (see Figure 8–6).

Figure 8–3: Three widths of cold tape – 6 mm (¼ inch), 9.5 mm (⅜ inch) and 25 mm (1 inch).

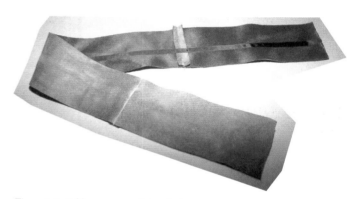

Figure 8–4: Cold tape on a waistband edge.

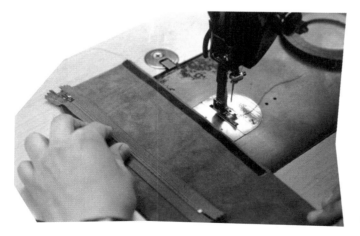

Figure 8–5: Cold tape on the stitching line of a zip.

Figure 8–6: Cold tape on the edge of a cuff.

CHAPTER 9
SEAM FINISHES

There are three types of leather seams, which take into account leather's non-fraying characteristics. The one you select will depend on the position of the seam and the type of leather you are stitching. In this chapter we look at these finishes.

SEAM OPTIONS

If you are a beginner sewer, you should not attempt to sew leather and suede. If you make a mistake, you will have great difficulty hiding your re-sewn areas. You may even ruin the garment entirely because ripping out the seams in a poorly sewn leather garment can damage the skins irreparably. This can become costly. Even if you are an experienced sewer, you should practise on leather or suede swatches before you tackle 'the real thing'.

You don't really need to finish leather edges since they do not unravel. You should generally allow a 9.5–12.5-mm (⅜–½-inch) seam allowance, unless your design requires otherwise. The only real exception to this applies to collars, where you should allow a 6–9-mm (¼–⅜-inch) seam allowance.

Although you don't have many edging options, you do have a few seam options. These are the three most common types of seams:
1. Open and glued.
2. Mock flat fell.
3. Raw edge lapped and stitched.

KEY

Right side of leather

Wrong side of leather

Previous spread: This black leather and astrakhan jacket with frog closures and stitching detail on the sleeves was included in Ralph Lauren's 1993 collection. It features open and glued seams.

OPEN AND GLUED SEAM

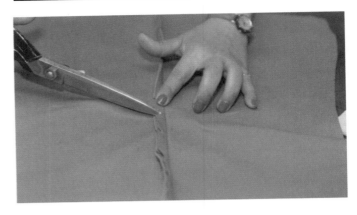

STEP 1

Stitch the seam. If the seam is curved, clip into the seam allowance no closer than 3 mm (⅛ inch) to the stitching line. If you clip any closer than this, the garment may tear when it is worn. Non-stress seams, such as collars and pocket flaps, can be clipped closer.

STEP 2

Using a small paintbrush, apply glue to the seam allowance and gently press the seam allowance open and flat.

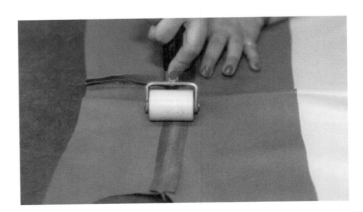

STEP 3

Apply pressure with a roller tool (see page 109) and roll the seams flat and smooth.

MOCK FLAT FELL SEAM WITH EDGESTITCH

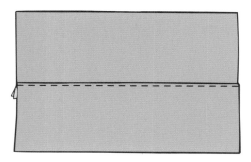

STEP 1

Stitch the seam. Push the seam allowances to one side and topstitch to the body

MOCK FLAT FELL SEAM WITH DOUBLE NEEDLE OR TRIPLE NEEDLE TOPSTITCH

STEP 1

Stitch the seam. Push the seam allowances to one side.

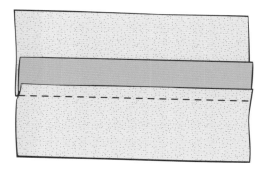

STEP 2

For double and triple needle seams, you may want to trim the seams as you sew them together. This, technique, often used on more expensive garments, results in a step effect and reduces excess bulk. To do this, sew the first edge stitch.

STEP 3

Trim the upper seam allowance by 6 mm (¼ inch).

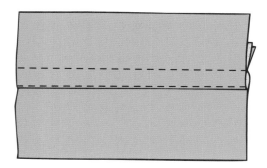

STEP 4

Stitch the second edge stitch to create the double needle effect, or a third edge stitch for a triple needle effect.

SINGLE RAW EDGE LAPPED AND STITCHED SEAM

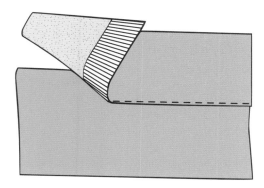

STEP 1

Start with a very even-edged seam. You may want to pink the edge for a decorative effect. Cold tape the wrong side on the edge to prevent stretching while topstitching. For a single stitched lap you will need a 6-mm (¼-inch) seam allowance. This will create an edgestitched effect.

DOUBLE RAW EDGE LAPPED AND STITCHED SEAM

STEP 1

For a double-stitched lap you will need a 12.5-mm (½-inch) seam allowance. Lap one seam over the other.

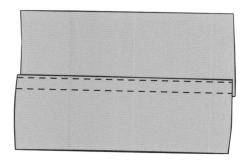

STEP 2

Topstitch 6 mm (¼ inch) from the raw edge.

CHAPTER 10
SEWING A SHIRT

A leather shirt takes much the same form as a shirt made from any other fabric. The key differences are some of the construction techniques and the joining of the smaller sections of leather to make the larger pattern pieces. This chapter covers the steps involved in constructing a shirt.

CONSTRUCTING A SHIRT

The construction techniques demonstrated in this chapter include collar and collar stand setting, facing applications, sleeve setting, lining insertion, pocket construction, seaming and topstitching.

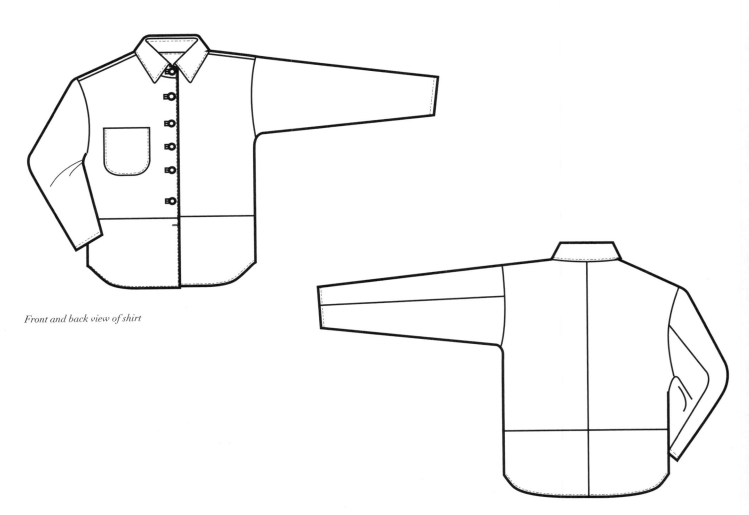

Front and back view of shirt

Previous spread: Country music star Willie Nelson is among the many celebrities who seek out the exclusive, hand-sewn pieces of Jordan Betten. Here Nelson wears a collarless shirt from 2004.

SHIRT PATTERN PIECES

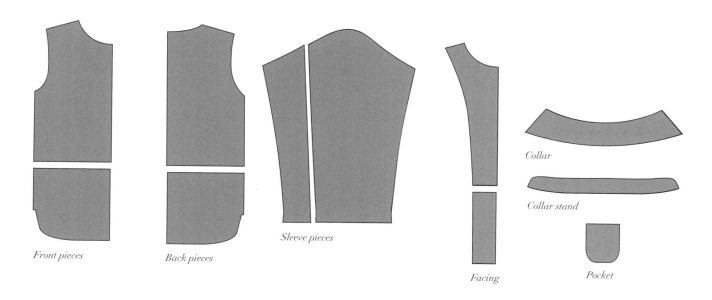

Front pieces

Back pieces

Sleeve pieces

Facing

Collar

Collar stand

Pocket

INTERFACING PATTERN PIECES WITH COLD TAPE

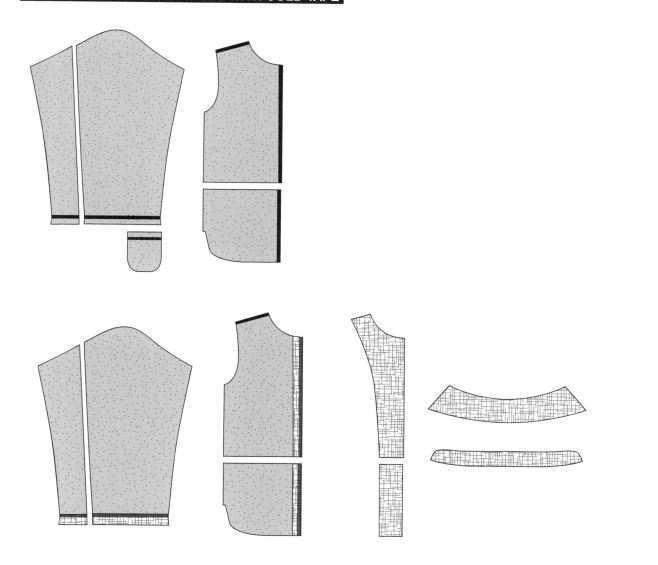

STEP 1

Cold tape the centre front panels, front shoulders, sleeve hems and pocket.

STEP 2

Interface the centre front, sleeve hem. Interface the collar, collar stand and front facing pieces (see pattern pieces on page 121).

STEP 3

Join together the upper and lower pieces of the front facings, shirt front and shirt back. Join the two-piece sleeve together. Glue open all the seams and roller them flat.

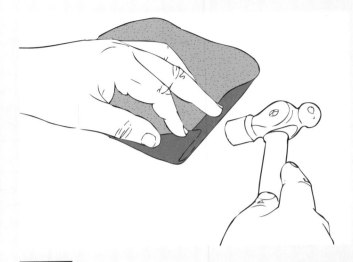

STEP 4

Prepare the pocket by gluing the seam allowance, bending it back and hammering the edge flat.

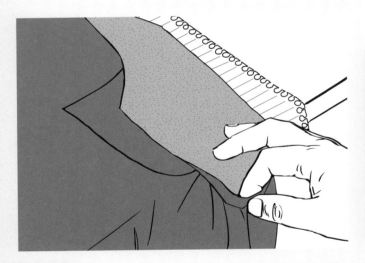

STEP 5

Place a piece of paper under the shirt front for ease when sewing the pocket to the body.

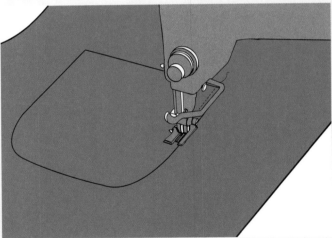

STEP 6

Stitch the pocket to the body. Do not backtack.

STEP 7

Pull the threads through to the wrong side and double knot them.

STEP 8

Join the shoulder seams together with cold tape, open, glue and roller flat.

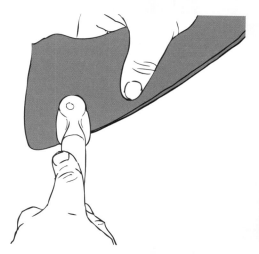

STEP 9

Sew the upper and under collar together, turn, trim, clip and hammer the edge flat.

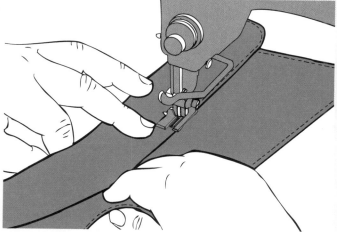

STEP 10

Stitch the collar together before setting it into the collar stand. Backstitch the collar stand.

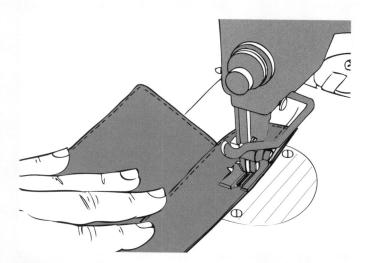

STEP 11

Stitch the collar stand together at the neckline.

STEP 12

Trim the ends of the collar stand before setting it into the neckline to avoid excess bulk.

STEP 13

Sew the lining and front facing together, then stitch the front and back shoulder of the lining.

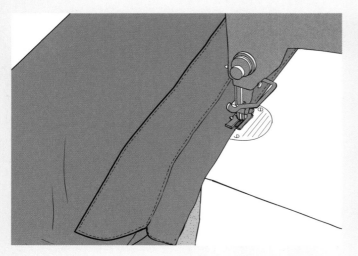

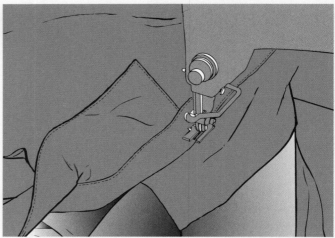

STEP 14

Join the collar, collar stand and neckline together.

STEP 15

Attach the front facing/lining to the shirt, beginning at about 7.5 cm (3 inches) down from the centre front. Stitch around the neck, then down the centre front.

STEP 16

Backstitch the facing all around the neckline.

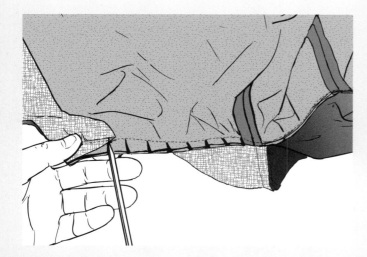

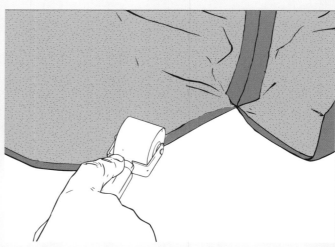

STEP 17

Thoroughly clip the neckline seam allowance.

STEP 18

Close the front and back side seams and sleeve inseams. Open, glue and roller flat.

STEP 19

Set the sleeve into the armhole and clip the seam allowance.

STEP 20

Glue and hem the sleeve. Topstitch, if desired. Glue the shirt seam allowance hem. Turn up and roller the hem.

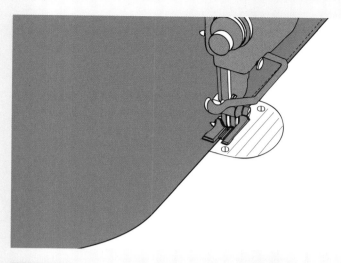

STEP 21

Edgestitch the front edge around the shirt hem. Make sure you have enough top and bobbin thread in the machine before topstitching.

STEP 22

Glue the facing to the body.

STEP 23

Sew the lining to the armhole. The armhole lining can be overlocked before stitching or a bias binding can be applied after attaching the lining to the armhole of the body.

STEP 24

If bound buttonholes are desired, they must be added before step 8 (see page 122). Also, refer to buttonhole instructions in Chapter 12, steps 1–7, pages 144–45,). Machine-made buttons or poppers (snaps) are also suitable. Buttons and button tacks should be hand sewn with a glover's needle.

CHAPTER 11
SEWING A PAIR
OF TROUSERS

Leather trousers can be made in as many different styles as trousers made from woven fabric. Like the shirt, the larger pattern pieces are usually assembled from more than one piece of leather and the assembling of the sections can be used to decorative effect. This chapter covers the steps involved in constructing a pair of pleated trousers, one of the most popular styles, incorporating elements common to other trouser styles, such as jeans.

CONSTRUCTING A PAIR OF TROUSERS

The techniques demonstrated here include the construction of the fly front, seaming, crotch sewing, zip setting, darts, pockets, pleats, lining, loops and waistband.

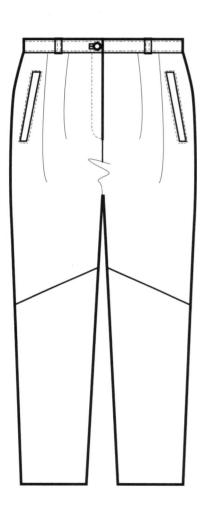
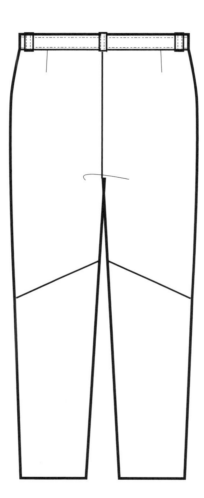

Front and back view of trousers

Previous spread: For this pink leather trouser suit from 1994, Vivienne Westwood created a pair of knee-length trousers, trimmed with a frill.

TROUSER PATTERN PIECES

INTERFACING PATTERN PIECES WITH COLD TAPE

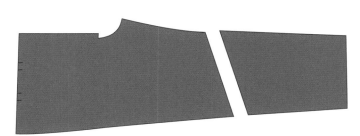

Top left, bottom left front trouser

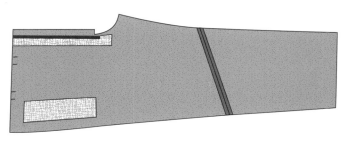

Top left, bottom left front trouser; stitched

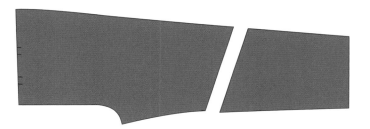

Top right, bottom right front trouser

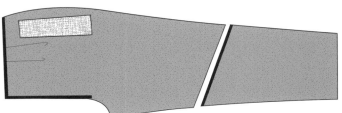

Top right, bottom right front trouser; not stitched

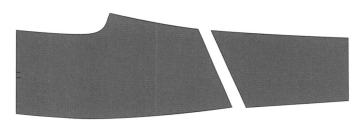

Top and bottom back trouser; not stitched

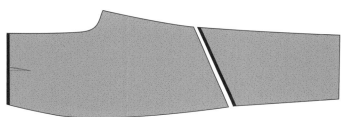

Top and bottom back trouser; not stitched

Waistband

Pocket welts

Fly extension

Fly facing

Belt loops (not cut)

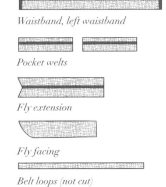

Waistband, left waistband

Pocket welts

Fly extension

Fly facing

Belt loops (not cut)

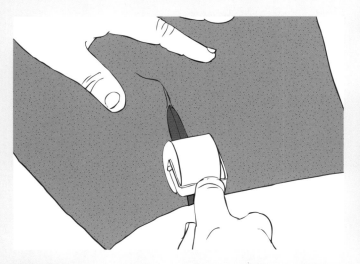

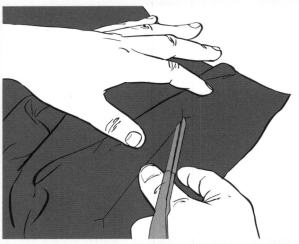

STEP 1

Sew the front pleats and sew the back darts, then glue open and roller flat.

STEP 2

Cold tape and interface the front and back waist, pocket welts, fly seam, fly pieces and waistband (see the pattern pieces on page 129).

STEP 3

Interface the waistband, fly front, pocket opening, welt and fly extension.

STEP 4

Prepare the pockets by slashing each pocket open and clipping into the corners.

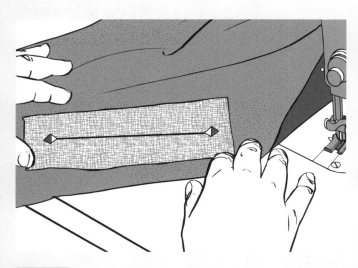

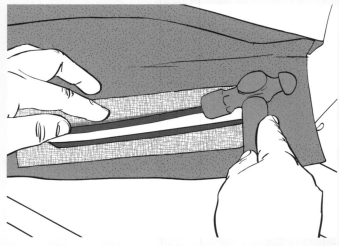

STEP 5

Glue the pocket seam allowances open.

STEP 6

Hammer the pocket seam allowances flat.

STEP 7

Prepare the pocket welt pieces and the fly extension by gluing them. Fold them in half and roller them flat.

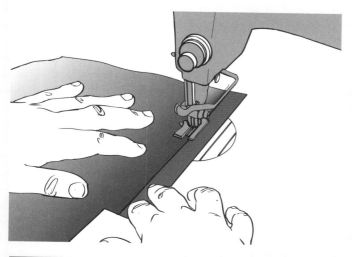

STEP 8

Attach the pocket facing and pocket welt to the pocket lining and backstitch each of them.

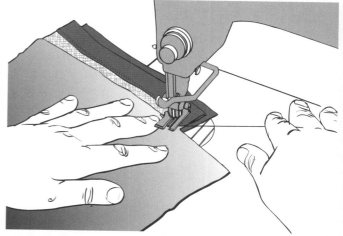

STEP 9

Stitch the upper and lower pockets together.

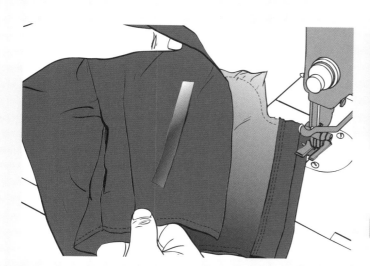

STEP 10

Place the trouser front over the pocket bag.

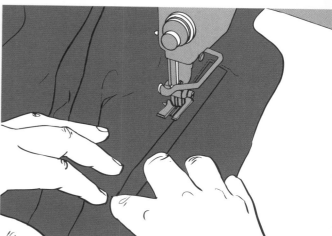

STEP 11

Fold down the lower pocket facing while topstitching the pocket welt to the trouser on three sides.

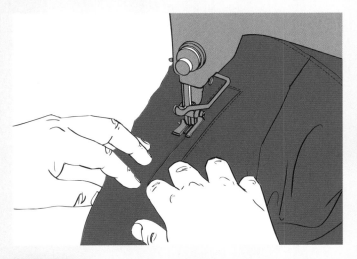

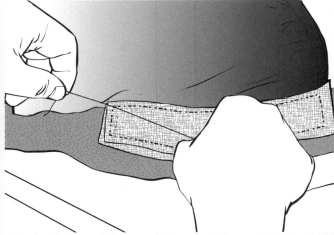

STEP 12

Flip the lower pocket facing up and topstitch the last side of the pocket to the trouser.

STEP 13

Do not backtack or clip threads after sewing this step.

STEP 14

Pull the threads through to the back and double knot. Complete the pocket by stitching the pocket bag top and bottom.

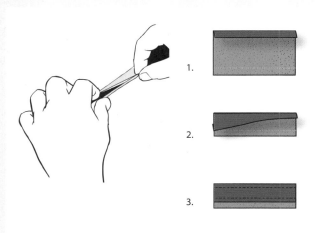

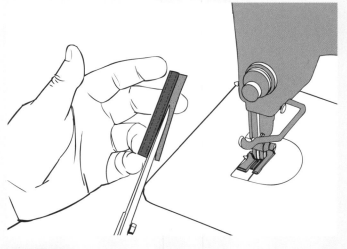

STEP 15

Prepare the belt loops by 1) folding over 6 mm (¼ inch), 2) folding again to make a 7.5-mm (⅜-inch) wide loop and 3) edgestitching the loop on the folded edges and pressing flat.

STEP 16

Trim the seam allowance close to the edge.

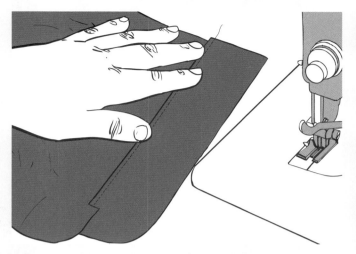

STEP 17

Sew the curved fly facing to the trouser.

STEP 18

Turn and backstitch the facing.

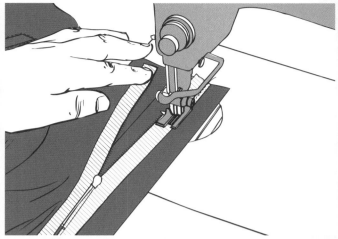

STEP 19

Sew the zip to the fly facing.

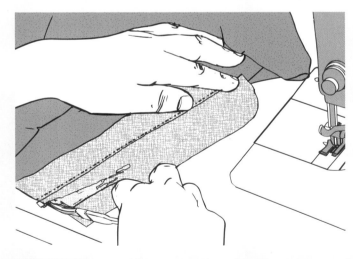

STEP 20

Glue the fly facing to the trousers.

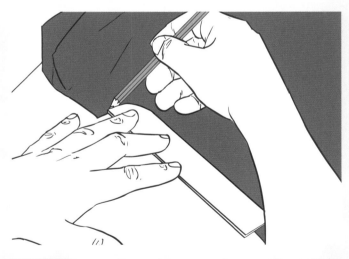

STEP 21

Using a template, lightly mark the topstitch edge with a pencil.

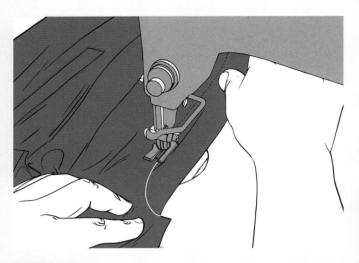

STEP 22

Topstitch the fly front along the marked line.

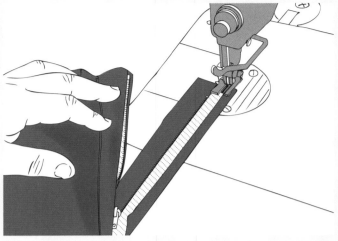

STEP 23

Stitch the zip to the left facing on the edge of the zip tape.

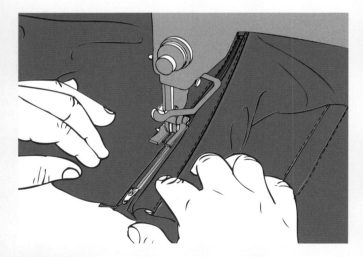

STEP 24

Starting at the base of the zip on the left side of the fly, turn back a 12-mm (½-inch) seam allowance and stitch the zip to the trousers close to the zip teeth.

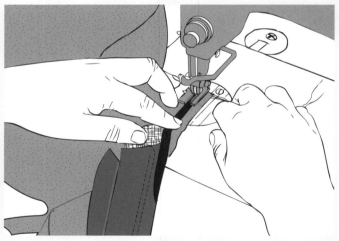

STEP 25

Cold tape the front crotch on one side while sewing the two fronts together, beginning at the crotch, to the base of the zip. Clip the crotch all around.

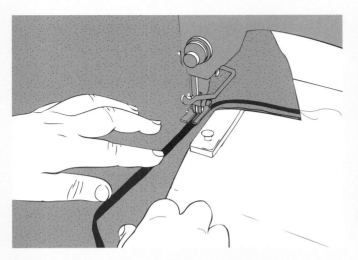

STEP 26

Cold tape and stitch the back crotch. You may wish to use a sewing guide attachment.

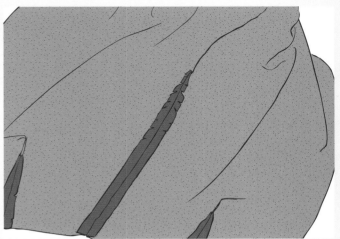

STEP 27

Clip the back crotch and glue the seams open.

STEP 28

Sew the side seams and inseams open, then glue and roller them flat.

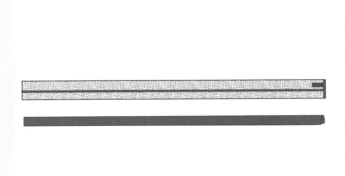

STEP 29

Make the buttonhole on the waistband (see Chapter 12, steps 1–7, pages 144–45). Glue the edges of the centre front seam allowance on the waistband.

STEP 30

Sew the lining together.

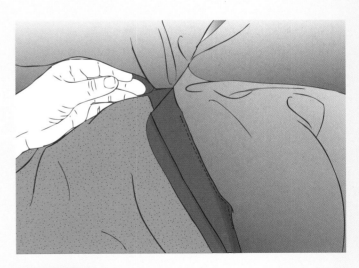

STEP 31

Attach the lining to the fly extension on the left side.

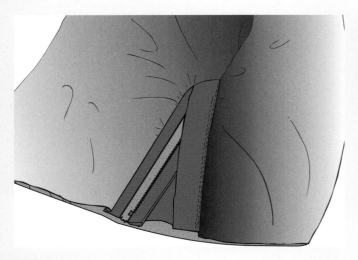

STEP 32

Attach the lining to the right side of the fly facing, catching the left side of the fly extension.

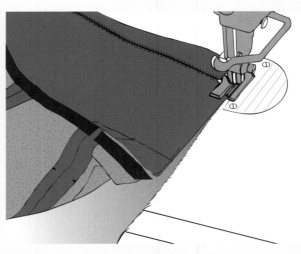

STEP 33

Stitch the lining to the trousers at the waistband.

STEP 34

Trim the edge on the waistband close to the seamline to eliminate bulk in this area.

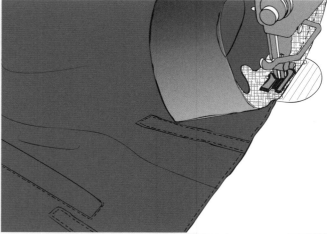

STEP 35

Align the belt loops to the waistband while joining the waistband to the trouser waist.

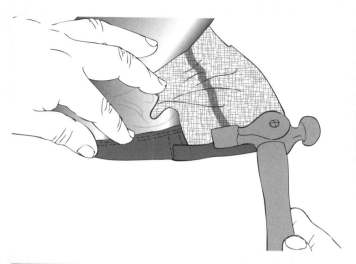

STEP 36

Fold over the waistband centre edge and hammer it flat.

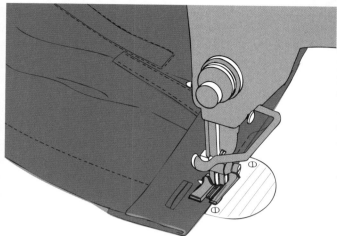

STEP 37

Beginning at the front belt loop, edgestitch the waistband all around.

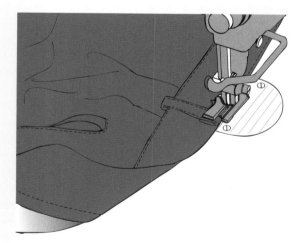

STEP 38

Catch the upper loop as you topstitch the upper edge of the waistband.

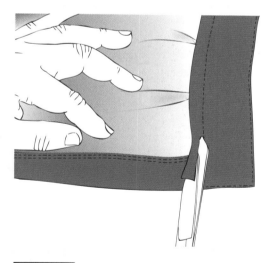

STEP 39

Trim the waistband seam allowance on the inside.

STEP 40

Machine topstitch the hem of the lining. Glue and turn up, or glue and topstitch the trouser hem. Sew the button on with a glover's needle, using a button tack reinforcement. Press well.

CHAPTER 12
SEWING A JACKET

Leather jackets are designed in a huge range of styles and require a wide variety of sewing techniques. By paying particular attention to certain construction stages, you can achieve a perfect finish. This chapter introduces some of the basic techniques for sewing a classic bomber style jacket.

CONSTRUCTING A JACKET

The instructions for this garment will teach you the construction techniques involved in making welt pockets, pocket flaps, bound buttonholes, tabs, notched collars and collar stands, and facings as well as sleeve settings and the insertion of a full lining. Making a jacket is a complex and long process, incorporating many key processes that can be used for many other garments. Here they are broken down into simpler subdivisions to help isolate key aspects.

KEY

Right side of leather

Wrong side of leather

Lining

Interfacing

Cold tape

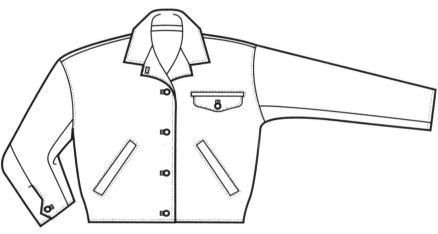

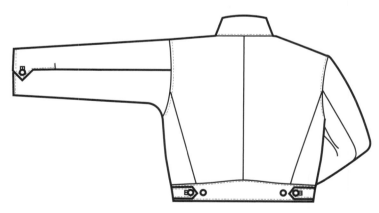

Front and back view of a jacket

Previous spread: Dior's head-to-toe leather statement in 1994. A tan shearling coat is worn over a suede shirt, paired with gloves and a tan leather skirt.

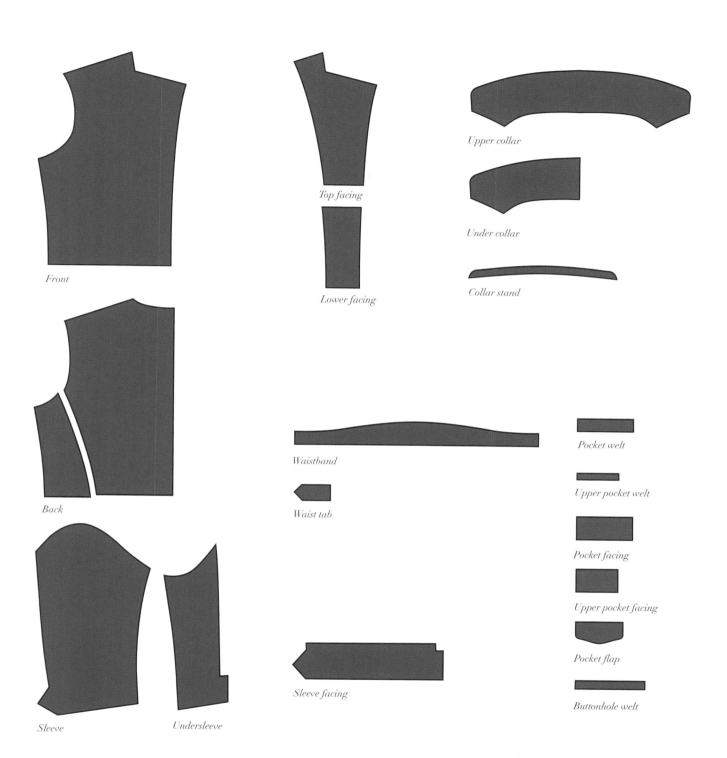

Front

Top facing

Lower facing

Upper collar

Under collar

Collar stand

Back

Waistband

Waist tab

Pocket welt

Upper pocket welt

Pocket facing

Upper pocket facing

Pocket flap

Buttonhole welt

Sleeve

Undersleeve

Sleeve facing

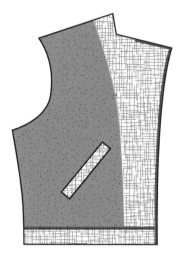

Left front

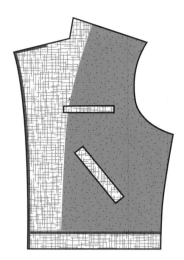

Right front

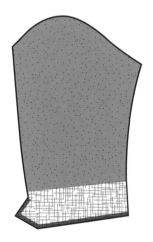

Sleeve

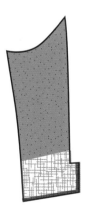

Undersleeve

Sleeve facing

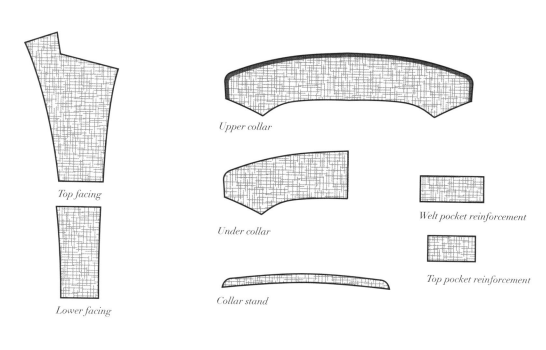

Top facing

Upper collar

Lower facing

Under collar

Welt pocket reinforcement

Top pocket reinforcement

Collar stand

Waistband (cold tape 1 piece only)

Waist tab

Pocket welt

Upper pocket facing

Upper pocket welt

Pocket flap

Pocket facing

Buttonhole welt

STEP 1

Cold tape and interface the jacket front and hem, upper collar, waistband (one piece only) and upper and under sleeve hem. Interface the upper collar, under collar, collar stand, pocket welts and facings, pocket flaps, waistband, waist tabs, buttonhole welt, front facings top and bottom, centre front body, front body pocket openings, upper and under sleeve hems and sleeve facings (see pattern pieces on pages 141–43).

STEP 1

Cut the buttonhole welt strip into separate welts. For a 6-mm (¼-inch) wide buttonhole welt, your pieces should be 25 mm (1 inch) long by 25 mm (1 inch) wider than the button. Fold each welt in half and then stitch in the middle. Next, join them together in pairs, 6 mm (¼ inch) away from the edge, with the folded edges facing each other. Fold open and hammer flat.

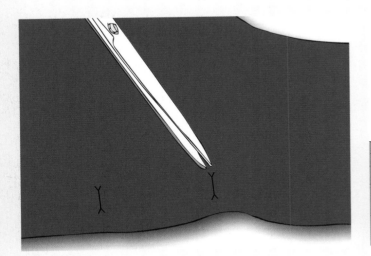

STEP 2

Slash each buttonhole open on all the pattern pieces (front body, pocket flap, tabs and sleeve hem), carefully cutting the 'V' at either end.

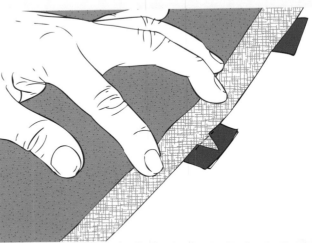

STEP 3

Turn the two 'V's at each end of the buttonhole to the wrong side and stitch to the buttonhole welt.

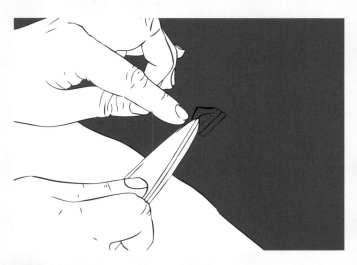

STEP 4

Turn under the two remaining sides of the buttonhole opening.

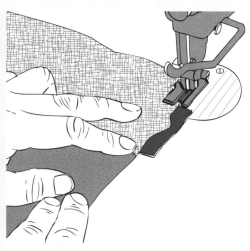

STEP 5

Stitch the two remaining sides of the buttonhole to the welt.

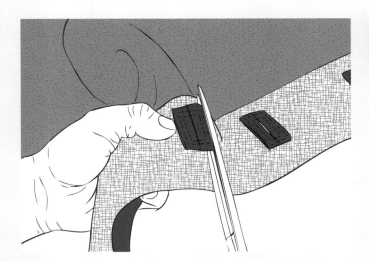

STEP 6

Trim the inside edges of the buttonhole welt.

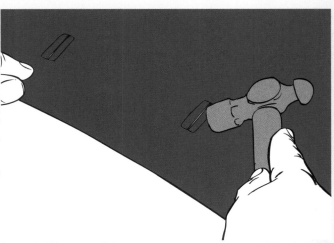

STEP 7

Hammer the finished buttonhole flat.

STEP 1

Using a template, mark the corners of the sleeve opening.

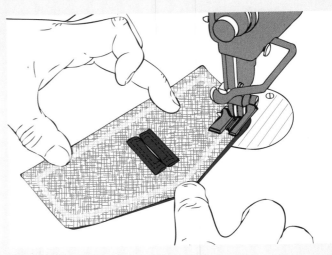

STEP 2

Using a template, mark and sew the pocket flaps.

STEP 3

Trim the under-flap pocket seam allowance in a stepways fashion and notch out the point.

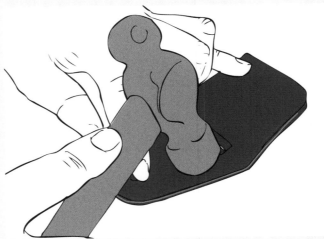

STEP 4

Turn the pocket and hammer its edge.

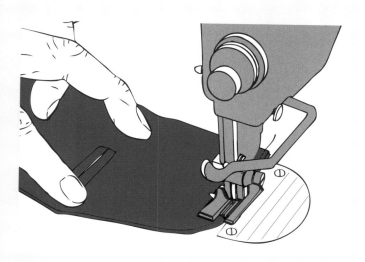

STEP 5

Edgestitch the pocket all around the flap.

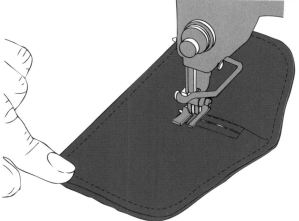

STEP 6

Crackstitch on the inside of the buttonhole.

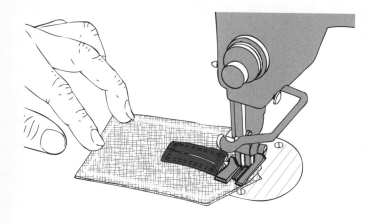

STEP 7

Using a template, mark, then stitch, the tab.

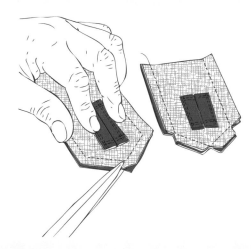

STEP 8

Notch out the points of the tab.

STEP 9

Trim, turn, edgestitch and hammer the tabs using the same technique shown earlier for the pocket flaps in steps 2 to 6.

PREPARE AND SEW THE POCKET WELTS

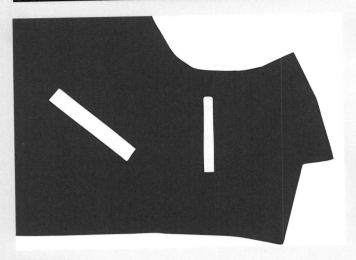

STEP 1

Iron the pocket interfacing reinforcement so that it is centred over the pocket slit on the wrong side. Slit the pockets carefully and glue them down (see Chapter 11, steps 4 to 5, page 130).

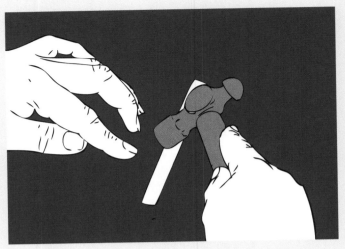

STEP 2

Hammer the pocket opening once glued.

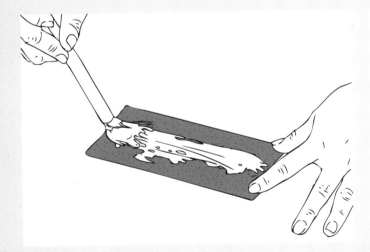

STEP 3

Prepare the welt by gluing the piece.

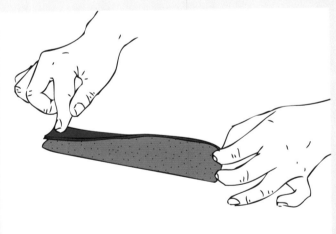

STEP 4

Fold the welt in half.

STEP 5

Hammer the welt flat.

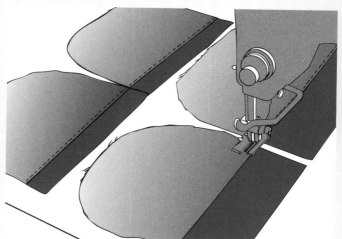

STEP 6

Sew the pocket facing and welt to the pocket lining and then backstitch.

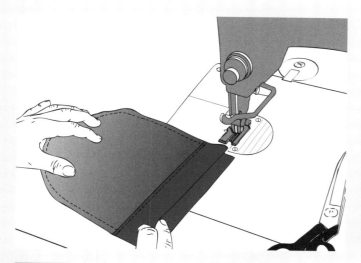

STEP 7

Join the pocket linings together, beginning at the welt seam allowance, to the same point on the other side.

STEP 8

Line up the pocket bag to the pocket opening, welt uppermost.

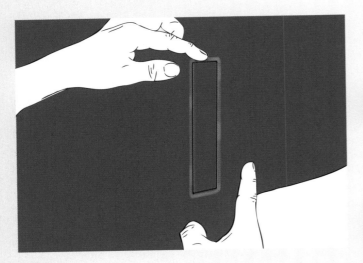

STEP 9

Position the welt so that the pocket opens from the top of the opening.

STEP 10

Starting in the corner, topstitch all around the edge of the pocket opening of the welt section. Be sure to fold down the pocket facing side first, then flip up to complete the topstitch.

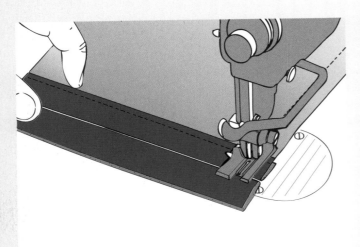

STEP 11

Prepare the upper pocket welts in the same way that you prepared the welt pocket, above (steps 3 and 4). Stitch one upper pocket welt and the upper pocket facing to the pocket linings in the same way as you did for the pocket (step 6). Join the two pocket welt pieces together by stitching them on the sides. Be sure to keep the underside of the pocket lining free.

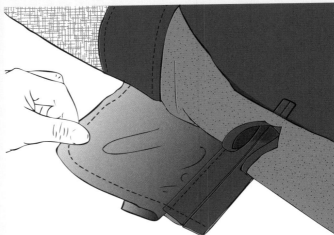

STEP 12

Place the pocket bag under the pocket opening in the body, with the welts aligned on the centre of the opening.

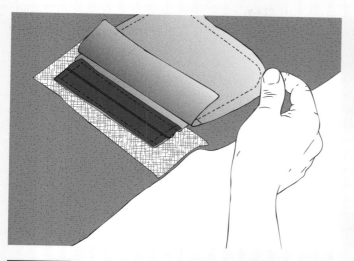

STEP 13

Be sure to fold down the facing side before stitching the lower side of the pocket.

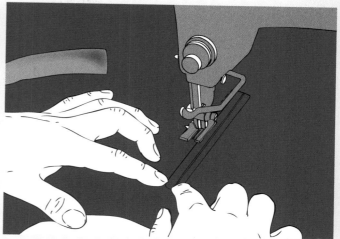

STEP 14

Start stitching in the lower pocket corner.

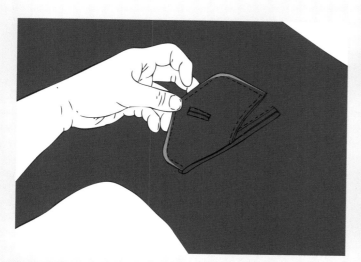

STEP 15

Insert the pocket flap into the upper pocket opening.

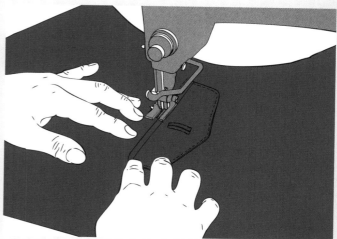

STEP 16

Continue to topstitch the top and sides of the welt. Be sure to flip up the pocket facing at this time.

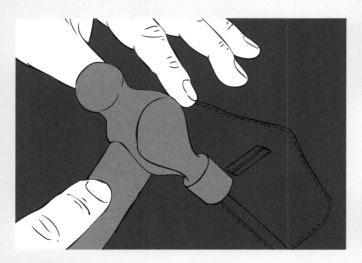

STEP 17

Hammer the pocket flap and upper pocket.

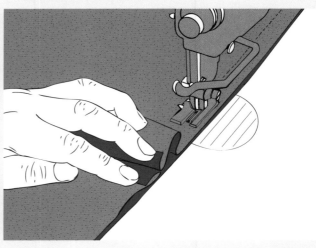

STEP 1

Join the centre back seam. Join the back waistband piece to the jacket back. Fold the pleat as you sew.

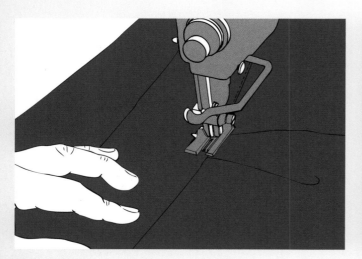

STEP 2

Join the waistband facing to the waistband and edgestitch on the waistband.

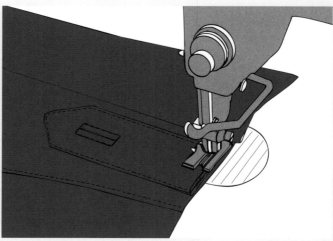

STEP 3

Place the tabs on the waistband side seam and stitch.

STEP 4

Close the side and shoulder seams.

PREPARE AND SEW THE COLLAR AND COLLAR STAND

STEP 1

Join the under collar pieces together.

STEP 2

Join the under collar to the collar stand.

STEP 3

Clip seam allowances on the collar stand and glue the seam open.

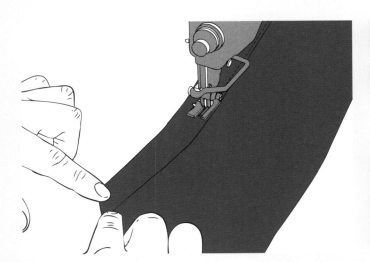

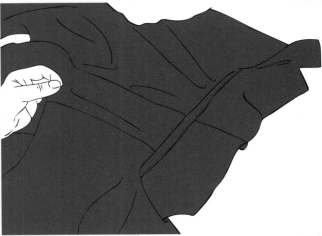

STEP 4

Edgestitch the collar stand.

STEP 5

Join the under collar to the body of the jacket. Stop 9.5 mm (⅜ inch) away from the edge of the collar.

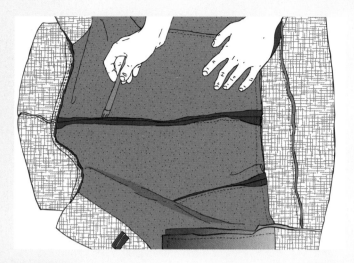

STEP 6

Glue all the inside seams open.

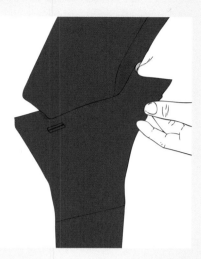

STEP 1

Sew the collar stand to the upper collar in the same way that you joined the collar to the undercollar earlier (see step 2, page 153). Join the front upper facing to the lower facing. Sew the collar to the front facing, leaving 9 mm (⅜ inch) open on each end of that seam.

SEW THE SLEEVE AND SLEEVE WRIST DETAIL

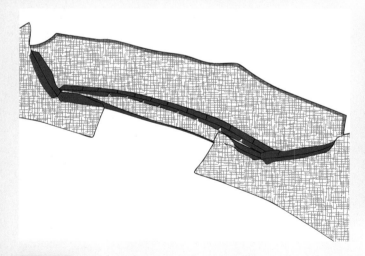

STEP 1

Clip, open, notch and glue the undercollar seam allowance and glue open all the corners.

STEP 2

Join the upper and under sleeve pieces together.

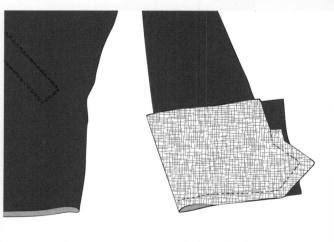

STEP 3

Sew the sleeve facing to the sleeve.

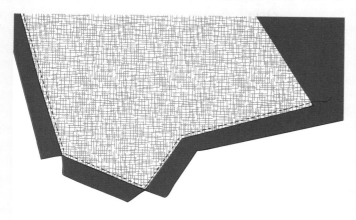

STEP 4

Clip and trim the sleeve facing in a stepways fashion.

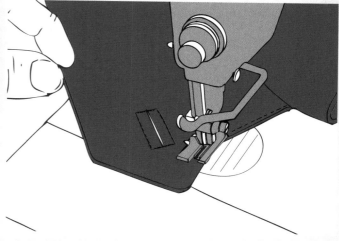

STEP 5

Turn, hammer and edgestitch the sleeve facing. Crackstitch the buttonhole.

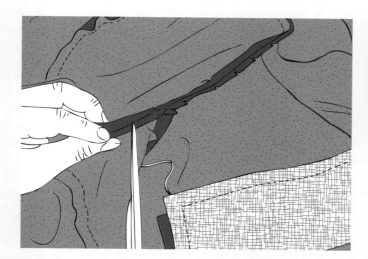

STEP 6

Sew the sleeve into the armhole. Clip into the seam allowance all around.

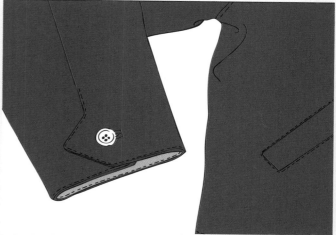

STEP 7

The completed sleeve.

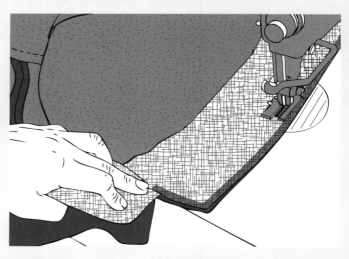

STEP 8

Stitch the shoulder pad to the shoulder seam.

STEP 1

Join the front facing to the hem, on one side only. Start sewing the facing to the body about 7.5 cm (3 inches) down from the lapel point. Continue to sew around the lapel, stopping at the collar neckline intersection, and backtack. Flip the seam allowance out of the way and continue to stitch the collar, repeating this step on the other end of the collar until you get to 7.5 cm (3 inches) down from the lapel point.

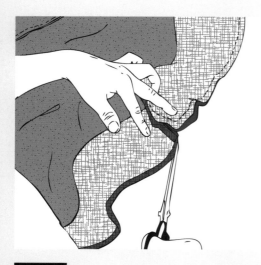

STEP 2

Compare both the left and the right fronts. Trim, if the lengths are uneven. Sew the facing to the hem and then complete the front facing. Clip the corners of the facing.

STEP 3

Trim the seam allowance of the facing in a stepways fashion.

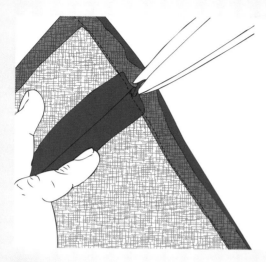

STEP 4

Trim the seam allowances on the hem/facing seam to reduce bulk.

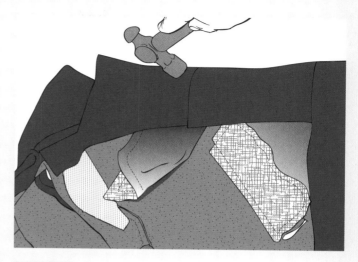

STEP 5

Turn the collar and facing. Hammer the collar edge and the front edge.

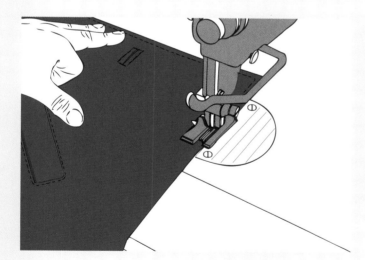

STEP 6

Sew a 6-mm (¼-inch) topstitch all around the edge of the jacket.

STEP 7

Sew the lining together. Leave a 25-cm (10-inch) opening in the sleeve inseam so the garment can be turned inside out later.

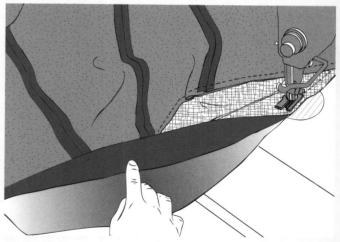

STEP 8

Join the lining to the body at the hem.

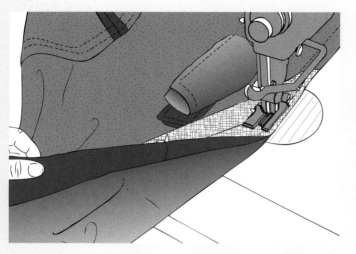

STEP 9

Join the lining from the hem to the top of the lapel on both sides.

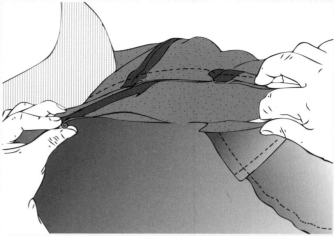

STEP 10

Sew the lining to the neckline.

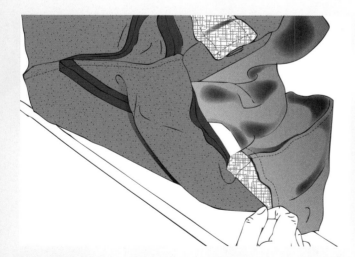

STEP 11

Sew the sleeve lining to the sleeve wrist opening.

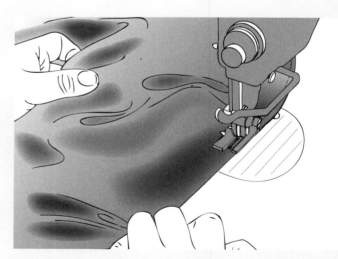

STEP 12

Turn the garment inside out and machine stitch the 25-cm (10-inch) opening on the sleeve lining inseam to close.

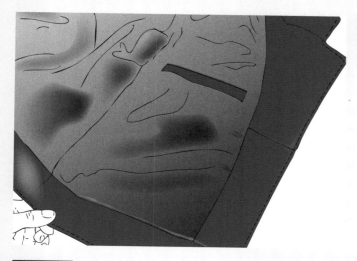

STEP 13

The jacket lining is complete.

MAKE THE BUTTONHOLES AND SEW ON THE BUTTONS

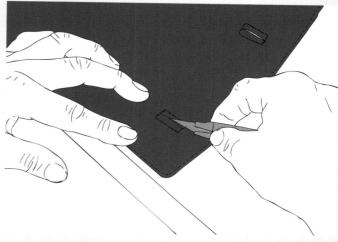

STEP 1

Slit all of the buttonholes with a short knife.

STEP 2

Sew the buttons together with a button tack reinforcement using a glover's needle.

STEP 3

Press the jacket well.

CHAPTER 13
LEATHER
DEFECTS

You can source garment leather from approximately 70 countries throughout the world. However, tanneries may send you skins with serious physical problems. This chapter advises on how to identify and solve many of the most common quality control problems encountered with finished, full-grain garment leathers and suede.

BASICS

When sourcing leather it is important to look at a wide range of quality control factors including the colour; strength and resistance to deterioration in wear from abrasion or environmental factors; shrinkage; stains including oil and water spotting; a white hazy deposit called spew or mould/mildrew; unpleasant odours; and, finally, defects in the grain.

THE IMPORTANCE OF INDEPENDENT TESTING

While many tanneries test their skins before they ship them to manufacturers, many others do not. You should make it a routine procedure to test the skins you buy before cutting them. Figure 13–1 shows an example of a leather test report.

One of the best testing labs in the world is the Leather Industries Research Laboratory at the University of Cincinnati. Much of this lab's experience is based on diagnosing problems with completed garments (as well as raw skins).

The Leather Industries Research Laboratory is one of the only independent leather testing labs in the United States. Many of the biggest leather garment manufacturers, as well as the top US retailers, send their skins or finished garments to this lab for testing. Frank H. Rutland, the lab's former Technical Director, has contributed most of this chapter's insights on leather testing.

You should also read *Skin, Hide and Leather Defects* by Jean J. Tancous for additional descriptions and illustrations of leather quality control problems and solutions.[1]

You should be aware that there are no consensus standards or industry specifications for garment leather in the United States. Product criteria are generally established between buyers and sellers through the evaluation and acceptance of initial production samples. Therefore, the recommendations made here are based solely on the quite considerable experience of the Leather Industries Research Laboratory, and should not be taken as representing definitive industry standards.

HOW TO IDENTIFY AND SOLVE KEY QUALITY CONTROL PROBLEMS

COLOUR PROBLEMS

FADING

Many people believe that fade resistance is relatively unimportant for garment leathers, since garment and product life cycles and exposure times are usually relatively short.

However, there are times when fade resistance can be quite important, for example for items that might need to be displayed for a prolonged period of time in a sunlit retail display window.

Frank H. Rutland reported that he once received a pair of black suede shoes. The right shoe had turned a reddish brown. His lab demonstrated that the colour alteration was due to light fading of a blue dye component in the leather. The lab speculated that the right shoe had been taken out of the box at some point in time for display purposes.

If you want to display an expensive leather garment in a sunlit window, you can check for potential fading problems by sending the garment to a lab. The lab will probably test the garment for fade resistance in a carbon arc or equivalent fadeometer. Ideally, the garment should demonstrate that it can endure a minimum of 24 hours' exposure with negligible colour change.

CROCKING

Crocking refers to the physical transfer of colour through a rubbing action. This can be a rather serious problem with some garment leathers.

To a large extent, tanners can minimize crocking by choosing proper dyes and effecting the right dyeing conditions when they process skins. However, since crock-fast dyes and dye fixation procedures are expensive, tanners may make compromises for the sake of economy. This is particularly true of some tanners outside the US.

Crocking can be tested under dry or wet conditions by rubbing the leather with a standard test cloth and then evaluating the degree of colour transfer using a standard chromatic transference scale (ASTM Method D 5053).[2] For good crocking resistance, testing labs look for values no lower than 4.0 dry and 3.5 to 4.0 wet, based on the AATCC Chromatic Transference Scale.

Suede leather poses additional crocking problems. Suede leather will not only transfer dye as described above, but can also transfer small dyed fibres that have broken off during suede buffing. Tanners can eliminate the problem by de-dusting their skins properly following buffing.

Previous spread: Josephus Thimister created this suede dress for his collection in 2000. Suede is prone to the physical transfer of colour when rubbed in a process called crocking. Leather can be tested for colour transference and the problem resolved by using crock-fast dyes.

TEST REPORT

KOREA MERCHANDISE
TESTING & RESEARCH INSTITUTE
459–28 Kasan-Dong, Kumcheon-Gu, Seoul, Korea
Tel: (02)856–5615–17, 19. Fax: (02)856–5618, 854–6667

DATE: 24 NOVEMBER 1995
NO.: 8121

CLIENT: KUMHUNG LEATHER CO., LTD.
SAMPLE DESCRIPTION: COWHIDE GRAIN LEATHER

TESTS CONDUCTED	RESULTS	TEST METHOD
DYNAMIC WATERPROOFNESS TEST		SATRA PM 34
– WATER PENETRATION (MIN)	17	
– WATER ABSORPTION (%)	52	
TENSILE STRENGTH (KGF)	17.2	BS 3144
TEARING STRENGTH (KGF)	6.8	BS 3144
SHRINKAGE TEMPERATURE (°C)	135	BS 3144
PH VALUE	3.7	KS M 6882
COLOURFASTNESS TO DRY CLEANING (CLASS)		BS1006 PART D01
– CHANGE IN COLOUR	4	
– STAINING (COTTON)	2	
COLOURFASTNESS TO RUBBING (CLASS)		BS1006 PART UK-LG
– DRY (200 CYCLE)	4–5	
– CHANGE IN COLOUR STAINING (WOOL FELT)		
– WET (50 CYCLE)	4–5	
– CHANGE IN COLOUR STAINING (WOOL FELT)	4–5	
COLOURFASTNESS TO LIGHT (CLASS)	OVER 4	AATCC 16A
SAMPLE		

Figure 13–1: Sample leather test report.

BLEEDING OR STAINING

This is the familiar problem that occurs when coloured and white items are mixed in the washing machine. It refers specifically to the migration of dye in solution out of the leather and onto another material. It is a condition that can be caused by perspiration, laundering or wet weather exposure, and is largely controllable by the tanner's choice of dye and dyeing conditions.

In order to anticipate the colour **bleeding (or staining)** potential of a garment, before your customers discover the problem for you, submit a sample of the leather to a qualified testing lab before manufacturing. The lab will probably test the skin by pressing the leather against a wet test cloth and then evaluating the degree of colour transfer (ASTM Method D 5552). Test results should be comparable to those for crocking resistance.

STRENGTH

In general, leather has exceedingly good strength properties. These properties make the material more than sufficient for most end-use applications. As a result, strength failures in leather articles are relatively uncommon.

However, since some garment leathers are quite thin, manufacturers can occasionally run into strength problems, particularly in the area of stitch tear strength.

One of the most common causes of low tear strength is **over-splitting**, where a thick hide is split into pieces of leather that are too thin. This is of particular concern with cattle hide garment leather. Most of the strength in an animal skin is in the interior (corium) of the skin, not in the outside or grain layer. If too much of the corium layer is removed during splitting, not only is the leather weakened but the hand and softness are also adversely affected. This condition can be detected microscopically if the thickness of the corium layer has been reduced to less than half of the leather's total thickness.

Stitch tear strength can also be measured directly (ASTM Method D 4705) but quantitative results are directly proportional to leather thickness. Considering this, the Leather Industries Research Laboratory hasn't identified a single desired test value that is independent of thickness. In general, the Leather Industries Research Laboratory believes that tensile strength (ASTM Method D 2209), which takes leather thickness into account, is a good surrogate test for most strength parameters. For garment applications, the Leather Industries Research Laboratory recommends a minimum tensile strength value of 1,134 kg per 6.4 sq cm (2,500 lbs per sq inch).

ABRASION RESISTANCE

In general, the abrasion or wear resistance of leather is quite good. For finished leathers, the actual level of abrasion resistance is to a large degree determined by the type of finishing system used on the skins and can be controlled to a reasonable degree by the tanner through the use of appropriate finish formulations.

For lightly finished or aniline leathers, there is very little that can be done to improve wear resistance. In garments made with such leather, excess wear is most likely to occur on turned edges (cuffs, hem lines, for example), where the leather is highly stretched and most exposed.

This property can be tested using a Taber Abrasion Tester (ASTM Method D 3384). With CS–10 wheels and 500 g (17½ oz) weight per wheel, the Leather Industries Research Laboratory looks for no evidence of finish wear (other than the possible dulling of the finish lustre) after 1,000 wheel cycles.

FINISH ADHESION

Finished leather, much like finished furniture, occasionally exhibits a problem with finish peeling or flaking. This is of particular concern with garment leather that will be subjected to a high degree of flex.

Poor finish adhesion is clearly a manufacturing problem that can result from improper finish formulations and high oil and grease content in the leather. You can easily test for finish adhesion by simply adhering a piece of sticky tape to the finish surface of a skin and then pulling it off sharply. If any finish is removed and remains adhered to the tape, you may be heading for a potential finish adhesion problem.

Finish adhesion can be measured quantitatively in the laboratory by adhering a test strip to the finish surface of the leather and then measuring the force required to peel the finish from the leather (European test method). This test is rarely performed in the US and there is no equivalent ASTM method at this time. More commonly, finish adhesion is determined by measuring

the flex resistance of leather. Although there are several test machines, one of the most common is the Bally Flexometer. Using this instrument, the Leather Industries Research Laboratory recommends that a skin stand up to a minimum of 60,000 flexes without producing visible finish cracks that permeate through to the surface of the leather.

BLOCKING

Another finish related problem is known as **blocking**, which is the adhesion of a leather finish to itself. Federal Test Method 3121.1 tests for this condition by folding a piece of leather and holding it together, grain-to-grain, under heat, humidity and pressure, so that the finish surface is in contact with itself. If the testing lab cannot separate the two leather grain surfaces without finish damage, the leather is said to block.

Blocking is also a finish formulation problem. It can be of particular concern in those applications, such as upholstery, where leather is likely to be in contact with itself under perpetual pressure and at elevated temperature and humidity. Blocking is a property of the finish top-coat system and is distinct from **tackiness**. Tackiness exists whenever leather feels tacky or sticky and will adhere to almost anything it touches. Tackiness is usually caused by inadequate drying or curing of the finish system.

It goes without saying that good garment leather should be free of blocking – in other words, when two pieces of finished leather touch each other, they should be able to be separated without damaging the finish.

CORROSION RESISTANCE

As discussed in detail in Chapter 2, the tanning process makes leather slightly acidic, with a pH of 5.0, sometimes less. This is quite normal and is not likely to cause any type of manufacturing or consumer problem. However, if the leather is too acidic, which occasionally happens, and is placed in direct contact with unprotected, corrodable metals (buttons, rivets, zips), the leather can corrode the metal.

To avoid this, the Leather Industries Research Laboratory recommends that leather pH should always be greater than 3.5 (ASTM Method D 2810). Also, corrodable metal trim (parts made of iron, copper etc.) should have some type of surface protection.

The corrosion resistance of leather can be measured directly by holding it in direct contact with a metal test block for a prolonged period of time at elevated humidity, and then observing if there is any test block corrosion (ASTM Method D 1611).

SHRINKAGE

One of the most common complaints that manufacturers and dry cleaners hear from their customers is that their leather garments have shrunk following commercial dry cleaning.

The cleaning industry has issued reports from testing laboratories that blame shrinkage problems on manufacturers' use of poor quality hides. In fact, shrinkage is exclusively a problem with the cleaning process itself. Specifically, shrinkage occurs when cleaners allow excessive temperatures and mechanical agitation to occur during the cleaning process. This is because leather protein fibres, like many textile fibres, are subject to shrinkage if exposed to high temperatures under wet conditions.

This fact must be taken into account when cleaning a leather garment. It is primarily for this reason that we strongly recommend that leather garment cleaning be done only by a qualified professional leather cleaner and not by an ordinary dry cleaner inexperienced in leather care.

OIL SPOTTING

Leather is a highly absorbent material. Because of this, leathers with little or no surface finish protection will readily absorb skin oil. Over time, this will darken the colour of the leather. This is particularly noticeable around the inside of a leather collar.

Unfortunately, oil spotting and soiling is particularly common in aniline and lightly finished leathers. These types of leathers generally require more frequent cleaning.

Manufacturers can avoid this problem by sewing in a protective lining inside the collar during garment manufacture. They may also avoid or minimize the problem by selecting skins that have been specially tanned. In recent years, new tannages have been developed that are highly oil and water resistant and even, in some cases, launderable.

There is also a number of customer-applied, leather care products on the market designed to provide a greater degree of oil-repellency in leather garments (see Resources as the end of this book).

SPEW

Occasionally, some leathers will develop a white hazy deposit on the surface. This deposit is known as **spew (or fatty spew)**. The condition is more likely to occur in colder weather and can be confirmed if the spew disappears after gentle warming.

Most leathers contain significant amounts of fat and oil, which act as natural lubricants for their protein fibres. In finished tanned skins, there will commonly be a combination of natural animal fat and the additional oils added by the tanner.

In soft garment type leathers, oil content may be as high as 20 to 30 per cent. Some of the fat and oil components that are not 'fixed' to the hide protein may migrate to the surface of the leather and solidify if their melting point is above ambient temperature conditions.

Spew usually appears as a hazy whitish film. Although it can be readily wiped away, it will probably redevelop in the right temperature conditions.

Gentle warming will cause the spew to melt and penetrate back into the leather. However, this solution is usually not permanent.

A light treatment with a suitable fat solvent can provide a more permanent solution. However, this should only be done by a trained professional since many solvents are quite toxic and there is a real danger of the solvents causing permanent damage to the skin's leather finish. The only way you can totally avoid spewing is to purchase properly tanned skins treated with an optimized oil formulation system.

MOULD/MILDEW

Leather's proteins and their associated fats and oils provide an excellent medium for fungal growth under damp conditions. Therefore, some care needs to be exercised during the handling and storage of leather garments.

Leather that has become wet should be allowed to dry slowly at room temperature without adding any heat artificially. Leather should be stored in a dry, well-ventilated area, and not under damp conditions (such as a damp basement), which is a sure invitation to mildew.

Leather should always be allowed to breathe and should not be stored in plastic garment bags. A garment bag can sometimes act like a greenhouse, providing the perfect conditions for mould or mildew growth.

Existing mould or mildew can easily be eliminated by wiping with a damp cloth, if caught early enough. You can correct more serious cases of mildew by spraying the skin or garment with a very fine mist of commercial fungicide. However, this must be done with extreme care to avoid spotting the leather or damaging the finish. Wherever possible, you should test such a treatment in a hidden area of the garment. If all else fails, the garment should be taken to a qualified professional leather cleaner.

WATER SPOTTING

Certain aniline or lightly finished leathers may be subject to water spotting. This condition will occur when the leather contains oils, dyes or other components that are water soluble. Once these components go into solution in water, they tend to migrate to the perimeter of the wetted area. When the leather dries, and the spotting components come back out of solution, they often leave a distinctly visible ring.

There is really very little you or your customers can do to solve this type of problem other than keep the leather as dry as possible. Some commercial after-care products that improve surface repellency may prove helpful, but these too need to be carefully tested in a hidden part of the garment as they may negatively affect the aesthetic properties of the leather.

As a manufacturer, you would probably be best advised to buy skins that have been produced using some of the newer oil and water resistant tannages.

ODOUR

The natural proteins in hides have very little odour. However, the oils and some of the processing chemicals used in the tanning process impart a characteristic 'leather' odour to leather goods. Generally, most people find this characteristic odour quite agreeable. Occasionally, however, customers may complain about bad leather odours.

Sometimes these complaints are simply due to the fact that some people are very sensitive to certain odours. However, some 'medicinal' leather odour problems are associated with the use of chlorinated phenolic preservatives during the tanning process. These additives are designed to prevent bacterial and fungal attack.

Although banned for use in the United States and Europe for over ten years, these materials are still legally available in other areas of the world and may be present in some imported leathers.

There is one other source of bad leather odour, which, although it is quite rare today, needs to be mentioned. The tanning process has evolved significantly over the years and most of today's tanners use entirely clean modern chemicals. However, this has not always been the case. Before the era of modern tanning, hides were treated with the natural enzymes found in animal excrement, a process known as **puering**. This process is still employed in some underdeveloped areas of the world and it is possible that some of these leathers have found their way into the stream of commerce, explaining the existence of an unpleasant leather odour in very rare cases.

LOOSE/PIPEY GRAIN

It is quite common for some garment leathers to evidence a **pipey grain**, a loose, coarse, puckered appearance on the grain surface of a skin. Severe cases result from the actual separation of the grain layer from the inner corium layer. This condition is known as **double hiding**.

Pipey grain can be caused by bacterial damage, excessive chemical treatment during tanning or the excessive mechanical working of the leather to produce a desired physical appearance.

Since garment leathers generally receive more chemical and mechanical treatment than shoe or leather accessory leathers to make them soft, they are more prone to pipey grain.

Some animal skins, such as sheepskins and goatskins, have a naturally loosely attached grain and are thus more prone to double hiding. Also, the belly and pocket areas of most skins have a looser fibre structure than other parts of the skin, making those areas more likely to becoming puckered.

Generally, the existence of pipey grain in a leather garment can be blamed on the manufacturer's poor purchasing and/or cutting decisions. A manufacturer can easily see, after a cursory examination, where skins are likely to pucker over time. If you avoid incorporating those areas in the raw skins in your finished garments, you will generally be able to avoid later puckering problems.

VARIATIONS IN APPEARANCE

Almost all leather products exhibit some variation in grain character (in full grain leathers), nap character (in suede leathers) and colour (in aniline leathers). These factors, along with surface blemishes, are natural variations that result from differences in the fibre structure within an individual hide or skin.

These differences tie to a specific location on the skin (such as the backbone or belly), animal breed, age, sex, feed and other environmental conditions and even seasonal factors. Variations in grain pattern, for example, are to cattlehide leather exactly what a 'cowlick' is to a human. Although such variations may be the bane of the leather cutter, they are part of what makes leather unique.

---

1 Available from the Shoe Trades Publishing Company.

2 References to standard test methods for leather in this chapter refer to either the ASTM (American Society for Testing and Materials) or Federal Test Method Standard No. 311 (General Services Administration).

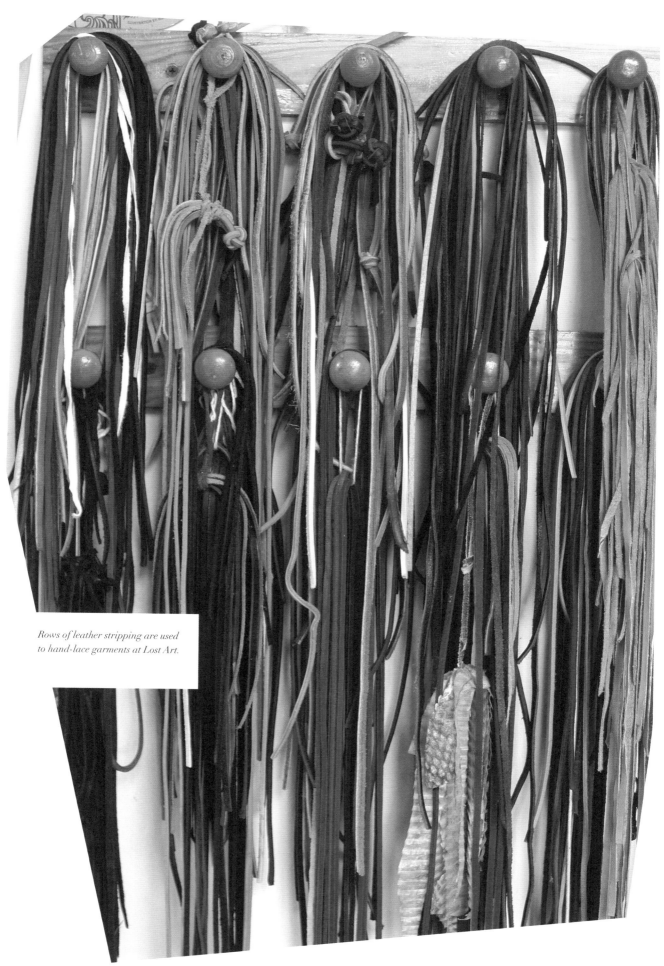

Rows of leather stripping are used to hand-lace garments at Lost Art.

CHAPTER 14
FAUX LEATHER

Like many fabrics, leather has its imitators made from synthetic fibres. Remarkably similar in their characteristics to their natural counterparts, faux leathers including faux suede, faux grain and faux patent leather are now seen on the catwalk. This chapter looks at the history, properties and the construction techniques particular to sewing these fabrics.

FAUX SUEDE, FAUX GRAIN AND FAUX PATENT LEATHER

For centuries, people have tried to mimic the beauty and luxury of leather. The earliest known attempts were by the Japanese who experimented with paper some 300 years ago. In 1870, Leatherette, a non-porous coated synthetic called polyvinyl chloride (PVC) over a fabric base, which, when embossed, simulated leather, was introduced. The early 1900s brought Naugahyde, made from polymer-coated plastic, called 'pleather'. Soon the name pleather was applied to any artificial leather product, but not all pleathers are the same. Polyurethane-coated pleathers are washable, can be dry cleaned and allow some air to flow through, while PVC coatings, in contrast, do not 'breathe' and are difficult to clean. PVC cannot be dry cleaned because the cleaning solvents can make it stiff.

Prior to World War II, American companies such as Goodyear and DuPont began offering faux shoe leather materials, but faux leather for garment making posed a greater challenge because the material needed to be soft. After seven years of research, Dr. Miyoshi Okamoto, a scientist at the Japanese company Toray Industries, developed a synthetic suede using advanced ultra-microfibre technology, and the result was a soft, breathable and wearable facsimile. Originally, Toray called the product Aquasuede, but six months later it was marketed in the United States under the brand name Ultrasuede®.

American designer Halston fell in love with Ultrasuede® at a dinner party where he spotted a shirt worn by Japanese designer Issey Miyake. Halston single-handedly catapulted Ultrasuede® into the fashion market the following season, in 1971, with his famous shirtdress, and later with his Braniff Airlines flight attendant uniforms, in 1977.

Ultrasuede® is washable, soft, colourfast and resistant to stretching and shrinking. It is available from Toray Industries in 37 colours.

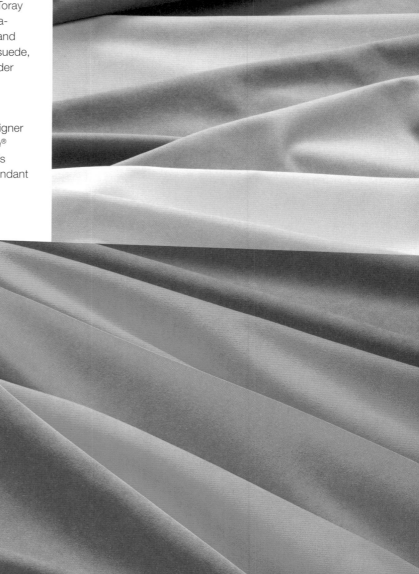

Previous spread: Baby Phat used Ultrasuede® for their autumn 2009 collection, in a wide range of jewel colours. This bright orange trench coat demonstrates the stretch and soft hand of the fabric.

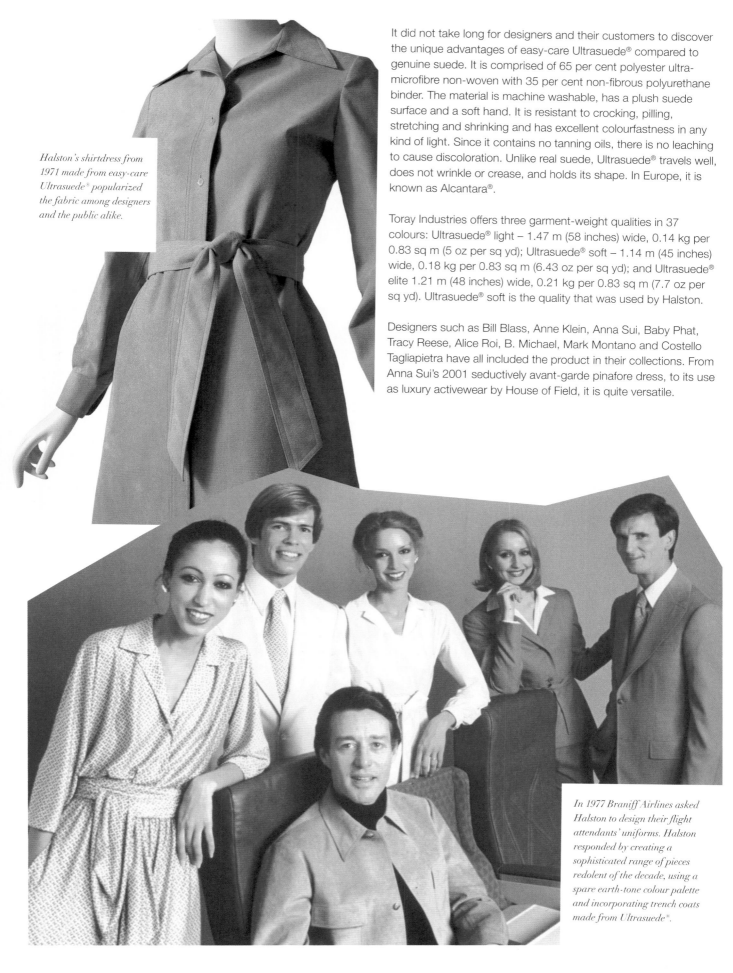

Halston's shirtdress from 1971 made from easy-care Ultrasuede® popularized the fabric among designers and the public alike.

It did not take long for designers and their customers to discover the unique advantages of easy-care Ultrasuede® compared to genuine suede. It is comprised of 65 per cent polyester ultra-microfibre non-woven with 35 per cent non-fibrous polyurethane binder. The material is machine washable, has a plush suede surface and a soft hand. It is resistant to crocking, pilling, stretching and shrinking and has excellent colourfastness in any kind of light. Since it contains no tanning oils, there is no leaching to cause discoloration. Unlike real suede, Ultrasuede® travels well, does not wrinkle or crease, and holds its shape. In Europe, it is known as Alcantara®.

Toray Industries offers three garment-weight qualities in 37 colours: Ultrasuede® light – 1.47 m (58 inches) wide, 0.14 kg per 0.83 sq m (5 oz per sq yd); Ultrasuede® soft – 1.14 m (45 inches) wide, 0.18 kg per 0.83 sq m (6.43 oz per sq yd); and Ultrasuede® elite 1.21 m (48 inches) wide, 0.21 kg per 0.83 sq m (7.7 oz per sq yd). Ultrasuede® soft is the quality that was used by Halston.

Designers such as Bill Blass, Anne Klein, Anna Sui, Baby Phat, Tracy Reese, Alice Roi, B. Michael, Mark Montano and Costello Tagliapietra have all included the product in their collections. From Anna Sui's 2001 seductively avant-garde pinafore dress, to its use as luxury activewear by House of Field, it is quite versatile.

In 1977 Braniff Airlines asked Halston to design their flight attendants' uniforms. Halston responded by creating a sophisticated range of pieces redolent of the decade, using a spare earth-tone colour palette and incorporating trench coats made from Ultrasuede®.

In addition to Ultrasuede®, Toray created a faux grain leather called Ultraleather®, comprised of 70 per cent cuprammonium rayon and 30 per cent nylon backing. In the mid-1990s Toray sold the rights to the patent to the American firm, Ultrafabrics, Inc.

From 1964, the Japanese firm Kuraray Co., Ltd. competed with Toray by creating their own version of faux leather known as Clarino®. Kuraray continues to market their faux leather under the trademark Amaretta®. Their grain leather is made from 55 per cent nylon and 45 per cent polyurethane and is 1.29 m (51 inches) wide in two garment weights: 200 g per sq m (7 oz per 1.19 sq yd) and 325 g per sq m (11¼ oz per 1.19 sq yd). Amaretta® is also offered in a faux suede version comprising 60 per cent nylon and 40 per cent polyurethane, available at 120 and 180 g per sq m (4¼ and 6⅓ oz per sq yd).

Throughout the years, numerous variations of faux leather and suede have entered the marketplace and at various price points. Generally speaking, more expensive products, such as Amaretta® and Ultrasuede®, are closer in appearance to the genuine article and are sometimes more expensive than using real leather. Some artificial leathers can fool even a leather expert. Companies such as Versace and Miu Miu, who traditionally work in real leather, have often dabbled in faux leather.

Another variation of faux leather is faux patent leather, created by applying a coating to the surface of a base fabric to mimic genuine patent leather. Genuine patent leather is often stiff and not as suitable for garment making as it is for accessories, which is why most designers choose to work in faux patent leather. While some designers use faux patent, as did Dolce & Gabbana for their 1995 collection of neon-coloured faux patent leather dresses, faux patent is most often used as outerwear for reasons of breathability. Genuine patent and faux patent leather can trap heat due to their synthetic surface layer, rendering such garments somewhat hot and clammy when worn close to the skin. Faux patent leather comes in a vast range of price points and is as popular in the lower priced market as it is in high fashion collections such as Emanuel Ungaro's 1988 collection of brightly-coloured faux patent leather jackets.

Faux leather is popular especially among designers who are committed animal rights activists. The PETA website offers consumers a list of companies that sell faux leather clothing and accessories. PETA also provides a materials resource directory to designers.

Anna Sui's windowpane check pinafore dress from 2001 shows the addition of pattern to Ultrasuede®.

Miu Miu reinterpreted a classic suit in mock croc leather in 1995.

The jewel colours of Ungaro's faux patent leather jackets from 1988 are combined with rich black velvet on the collars to create a sensuous collection of garments.

The relatively simple design of these faux patent leather dresses from Versace's 1994 collection works well with the characteristics of the material. The pared-back design will make the dresses more comfortable to wear in what is essentially a man-made fabric that will not breathe.

CONSTRUCTION TECHNIQUES

Careful fabric planning, cutting and sewing are essential when constructing garments in faux leather.

FABRIC REQUIREMENT

Faux suede behaves much like a nap fabric such as velvet. You need to plan your cuts so that your pieces match the direction of the product's natural nap. Faux grain and patent leather, on the other hand, can be cut both ways, so you can plan as for any non-nap fabric.

CUTTING

Faux suede must always be cut in the same direction with the nap smooth side down. However, you may wish to cut with the nap up for a darker, richer look, and with the nap down for a lighter, shinier look. All pattern pieces must be placed in the same direction. Faux suede has a slight stretch in the cross grain. Faux grain and patent leather can be cut in either direction. You can use pins on faux suede but not on faux grain and patent leather. Therefore, it is best to use weights to hold the pattern down on the faux grain and patent leather. If you must pin, pin only in the seam allowance since all pinholes will be permanently visible. Faux suede, grain and patent leather can be cut with scissors or a rotary cutter. The fabric can be cut while folded using weights, although you will get a better yield when you cut with the fabric open.

MARKING

For marking, use smooth tailor's chalk and/or a chalk or light lead pencil. Avoid using a tracing wheel, as this will perforate the material. You may also make a small hole when marking dart points.

BASTING

All basting must be done in the seam allowance since needle holes will remain in faux suede, faux grain and patent leather. You should use fine pins. You can also use double-sided tape, but do not use glue of any kind.

SEAMS

Seam allowances are usually 9 mm (⅜ inch), except for any pattern pieces that are turned and trimmed or cleaned, such as collars, pocket flaps and epaulettes. For the latter pieces, use a 6-mm (¼-inch) seam allowance.

Faux suede, faux grain and patent leather edges will not fray. Therefore, it is not necessary to finish the edges.

When sewing seams, be careful not to make your stitches too small as they will cause the seams to rip.

TABLE 14–1 STITCH LENGTH AND NEEDLE SIZE

	Fabric Needle Size	Topstitch Needle	Stitch Length	Topstitch Length
FAUX GRAIN & PATENT LEATHER	#9-11 BALLPOINT	#9-14	8-10 STITCHES PER 2.5CM (1 INCH)	6-8 STITCHES PER 2.5CM (1 INCH)
FAUX SUEDE	#11-14	#11-16	8-10 STITCHES PER 2.5CM (1 INCH)	6-8 STITCHES PER 2.5CM (1 INCH)

In 1994, the same year that Versace produced his 'safety-pin' dress, famously worn by Elizabeth Hurley, he designed this faux leather cut-out dress, apparently fastened together with large gilt buttons.

SEAM FINISHES

There are three basic seam construction methods to choose from when sewing with faux suede, faux grain and patent leather:

1. The conventional seam.
2. The topstitched seam.
3. The lapped seam.

THE CONVENTIONAL SEAM

Here, the seam is sewn, opened and pressed flat on the wrong side using a pressing cloth or a pounding block (see Figure 14–1).

Sometimes, it may be necessary to use a strip of double-sided fusible web (such as Stitch Witchery) to hold the seams down flat (see Figure 14–2 and Figure 14–3).

KEY

Right side of leather　　*Wrong side of leather*

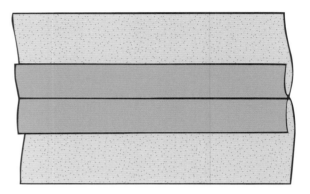

Figure 14–1: Conventional seam sewn, opened and pressed flat.

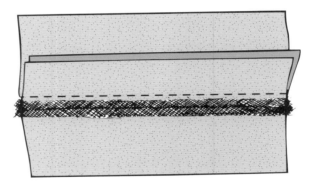

Figure 14–2: Placing double-sided fusible strip to hold seams down.

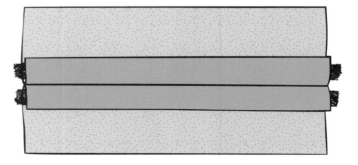

Figure 14–3: Double-sided fusible web holding seams down.

THE TOPSTITCHED SEAM

Here, the seam is sewn, opened and topstitched flat (see Figure 14–4). Alternatively, the seam is sewn, then one side is trimmed to create a graded seam effect (see Figure 14–5). Or, all of the seam allowance is placed to one side and then topstitched (see Figure 14–6).

Always be sure that you have enough thread in the bobbin as well as on top of the machine before beginning any topstitching.

THE LAPPED SEAM

Here, the raw edge is placed on top of the seam allowance and then topstitched for a sporty effect. Be sure to cut your edges accurately as uneven edges do not look good (see Figure 14–7).

Sometimes designers like to use a combination of seam finishes in the same garment, especially since crotch seams and armholes look better when sewn with a conventional seam finish. You can also use a pair of pinking shears to add a decorative touch to your raw edge.

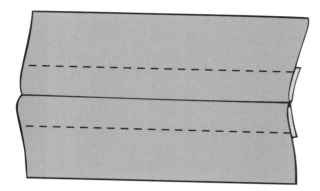

Figure 14–4: Seam opened and topstitched.

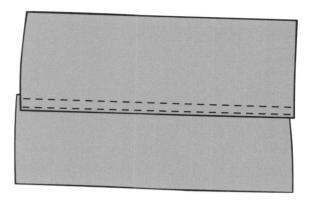

Figure 14–7: Lapped seam effect.

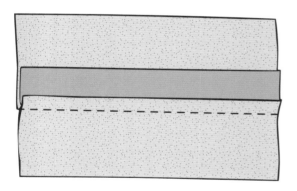

Figure 14–5: Graded seam effect.

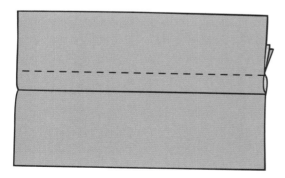

Figure 14–6: All of the seam allowance is placed to one side, then topstitched.

HEM FINISHES

Faux leather and suede can be hemmed using one of four methods:

1. Raw edge.
2. Turned up and machine topstitched.
3. Turned up and handstitched.
4. Turned up and held in place with a double-sided fusible strip.

THREAD

The best thread choice for all faux leather and suede products is either 100 per cent polyester or a cotton-wrapped polyester. For topstitching, two threads can be used, but always make a test swatch first.

INTERFACING

Use a preshrunk fusible interfacing. Make sure you fuse the interfacing to the wrong side of the fabric and that the grainy glue side is face down.

SPECIAL SEWING NOTES

Sewing faux leather and suede is similar to sewing the genuine article. However, certain techniques should be utitlized, especially when using a home sewing machine – faux leather and suede will not pass through the machine as easily as would a woven textile.

· A Teflon® sewing machine foot, plate and teeth may be useful in helping the fabric glide through the machine (see Figure 7–4, page 108). You may want to use your even-feed or 'walking foot' attachment if your sewing machine comes with one (see Figure 7–1, page 108).

· Placing a piece of tissue or loose-leaf paper between your garment and the machine tabletop while stitching will also help the material glide through the machine with ease. This technique is especially helpful when applying patch pockets (see step 5, page 122). When you are finished sewing, simply tear the paper away from the seam.

· Keep the machine top and bobbin tension eased. If you encounter skipped stitches try a new needle. If your machine skips when sewing over thick seams, place a small piece of cardboard or a folded piece of paper or fabric at the back end of the presser foot to level it with the thicker seam, removing the paper when you have finished sewing the thick seam.

· Choose patterns and designs that are tailored and avoid styles with a lot of gathers and fullness. Faux suede, grain and patent leather can only be eased about 2.5 cm (1 inch) in 25 cm (10 inches).

· Don't use too many darts and make them as long as possible. Avoid dimpling at the point by trimming the fabric on the inside of the dart down to the point. It is best not to backtack the dart points but rather tie a knot at the end points. You may use a dab of fray prevention solution on the end to hold the knot (see Figure 14–8).

· Reinforce dart points and crotch seams with a small piece of fusible interfacing.

· To remove any unwanted pinholes in faux suede, steam press the garment and then brush it with a brush to raise the nap and shrink the hole.

· Faux grain and patent leather will show holes, so avoid having to rip open seams.

LINING

Lining can be used to prevent the garment from stretching, to hide the inside construction of the garment or to provide comfort. If you decide to add a lining, make sure you use a washable lining if you want the garment to be washable.

PRESSING

You should iron a faux suede or faux leather garment on a low synthetic setting.

For faux suede, a reflective ironing board cover will cause shine so always press on the wrong side with a napped pressing cloth, a piece of terry towelling, or another piece of faux suede between the ironing board and the material. Put strips of paper under the seam allowance to prevent an imprint on the right side.

Faux grain and patent leather can be pressed with a pressing cloth or a piece of brown paper on the top or on the wrong side. You may press using light steam but be careful that the iron doesn't drip.

Using a pressing ham, a roller tool and a presser's mitt will also be helpful, especially when ironing curved seams (see Figure 14–8).

CARE AND CLEANING

Recommended care instructions for faux suede and grain leather follow:

Machine wash/delicate cycle. Tumble dry/low setting, remove immediately. Use mild detergent without bluing agents. Do not bleach. Hand wash/hang dry. Do not wring or twist. Wash separately to avoid colour absorption from other garments. Brushing lightly will restore the nap.

Faux patent leather should not be machine washed as the surface will peel or crack. It is best to either dry clean the garment or simply wipe the outer surface down with a cloth and light soap and water. Faux suede and grain leather can also be dry cleaned if you prefer.

Faux suede, faux grain and patent leather can be stored in plastic bags, unlike genuine leather garments. Store garments on padded or wooden hangers as you would any fine garment.

Figure 14–8 (clockwise from top left): Pressing hams, presser's mitt, roller tool, marking chalk and pencil, scissors and rotary cutter, double-sided fusible web, walking foot attachment and fray prevention solution (centre).

RESOURCES

TIPS FOR PROPER LEATHER GARMENT CARE

A leather garment should be treated as you would any fine garment with a few exceptions:

1. Do not store the garment on a wire hanger. Always use a wide hanger to maintain the garment's shape.

2. Do not store leather garments in plastic bags or in a hot, bright or damp room. Excess dryness may cause the leather to crack and moisture can cause mildew. You should consider cold storage during the summer months.

3. If your leather garment gets wet, allow it to air dry naturally since quick drying near a radiator will cause the leather to dry out and crack.

4. A new leather garment can be pre-treated with a stain repellent finish which will help prevent stains from occurring.

5. Leather cleaners and conditioners are available in retail outlets to help restore leather garments to their original state after repeated wearing. However, an excess build up of these products can clog the pores in the leather, inhibiting the ability of the skin to breathe. Light cleaners and conditioners that are effective and easy to use are available. Note: all cleaners should be tested for staining on a small hidden area of the garment, for example near the hem or under the collar.

6. Do not apply pins or adhesive tape to the surface of a leather garment.

7. Avoid spraying perfume and hairspray directly onto a leather garment. In general, do not allow your garment to become very soiled as this may cause permanent damage.

8. Do not attempt to remove difficult stains yourself. Contact a qualified, professional leather cleaner.

9. A hem can be fixed by applying a small amount of rubber cement to it.

10. You can iron a leather or suede garment by placing heavy brown paper on it and using a low setting on the iron, with no steam.

11. Expect some colour and texture changes after professional dry cleaning, even when carried out by qualified professionals.

12. Garments may shrink after professional dry cleaning but will stretch out again with wear.

13. Wipe off dust and dirt on a leather garment with a soft dry sponge or cloth. Buy a special suede brush and buffing block to clean the surface of nubuck and suede.

14. Only trust a professional leather dry cleaner to clean your leather garment.

15. Do not send your leather garments to your local dry cleaner unless he can demonstrate that he cleans large volumes of these garments on a regular basis. Most dry cleaners know a lot more about textiles than leathers.

16. Women should consider wearing scarves when wearing very delicate, difficult-to-clean leather garments. Scarves protect garments from cosmetics and body oils.

17. If you would like to remove a small, minor stain yourself, try a large pencil rubber. Only do this after you've tested the process on the inner, unexposed facing of the garment to make sure that the rubber doesn't damage the skin.

18. If a garment becomes wrinkled, put it on a hanger and gently pull the wrinkles out without significantly stretching the skin. If this fails, try to press the garment with an iron. First, make sure that the garment is totally dry. Place heavy brown paper over the garment and keep the iron moving constantly over the paper. Set the iron on its lowest heat setting when you do this. Never use steam when ironing leather.

Previous spread: A line-up of Lost Art's handmade leather trousers.

DIRECTORY

TRADE ORGANIZATIONS

Africa
Ethiopian Leather Industries Association (ELIA)
www.elia.org.et

Eastern and Southern Africa Leather Industries Association (ESALIA)
www.africaleather.com

China
China Leather Industry Association (CLIA)
wwww.chinaleather.org

Europe
The European Leather Association OR Confederation of National Associations of Tanners and Dressers of the European Community (COTANCE)
www.euroleather.com

Members:
Bulgaria (BULFFHI)
Finland (SLIA)
France (FFTM)
Germany (VDL)
Greece (HTA)
Italy (UNIC)
Lithuania (LOGVA)
Netherlands (FNL)
Norway (NGL)
Portugal (APIC)
Romania (APPBR)
Spain (CEC-FECUR)
Sweden (SG)
Switzerland (VSG)
United Kingdom (UKLF)

European Trade Union Federation: Textiles, Clothing and Leather
www.etuf-tcl.org

France
Federation Française de la Tannerie Mégisserie (FFTM)
www.leatherfrance.com

Societe Internationale du Cuir S.A. (SIC)
www.sicgroup.com

Germany
Verband der Deutschen Lederindustrie (VDL)
www.vdl-web.de

India
Council For Leather Exports India (CLE)
www.leatherindia.org

India Trade Promotion Organisation
www.indiatradefair.com

International Textile, Garment and Leather Workers' Federation (ITGLWF)
www.itglwf.org

Italy
Unione Nazionale Industria Conciaria (UNIC)
www.unic.it

Associazione Italiana Pellettieri (AIMPES)
www.aimpes.com

Instituto di Certificazione per l'industria Conciaria (ICEC)
www.leonet.it/leather/icec

Netherlands
Federatie van Nederlandse Lederfabrikanten (FNL)
www.lederfabrikanten.nl

Norske Garveriers Landsforeningen (NGL)
www.aarenes.no

Portugal
Assoc. Portuguesa dos Industriais de Curtumes (APIC)
www.leatherfromportugal.com

Spain
Confederación Española de Curtidores (CEC-FECUR)
www.leather-spain.com

Switzerland
Verband Schweizerischer Gerbereien (VSG)
www.leder-gerbereien.ch

Turkey
Turkish Leather Council (TLC)
www.turkishleather.com

United Kingdom
British Leather Confederation (BLC)
www.blcleathertech.com

UK Leather Federation (UKLF)
www.ukleather.org

United States
Leather Industries of America
www.leatherusa.com

Leather Research Laboratory, University of Cincinnati
www.leatherusa.org

Leather Apparel Association
www.leatherapparelassociation.com

LEATHER TRADE FAIRS

Africa
All-African Leather Fair (AALF) (Addis Ababa)
www.allafrica.com

China
China International Leather Fair (Whenzhou)
www.donnor.com/leather

China Leather Exhibition (CLIA) (Shanghai)
www.chinaleather.org

Haining International Leather Fair
www.business-in-Asia.com/china_leather.html

China Fur & Leather Product Fair (Beijing)
www.fur-fair.com

China International Clothing & Accessories Fair (Beijing)
www.chiconline.com.cn

Lineapelle/Asia (Guangzhou)
www.lineapelle-asia.com

All China Leather Exhibition (ACLE) (Shanghai)
www.aplf.com

Columbia
Columbia International Footwear & Leather Show (Bogota)
www.ifls.com.co

Czech Republic
Styl International Fashion Fair (Brno)
www.bvv.cz/styl-gb

France
Le Cuir à Paris
www.lecuiraparis.com

Le Salon de la Maroquinerie (Paris)
www.ff-maroquinerie.fr

Pret à Porter (Paris)
www.pretparis.com

Germany
Igedo (Dusseldorf)
www.igedo.com

Hong Kong
Asia Pacific Leather Fair
www.aplf.com

India
India International Leather Fair (Chennai)
www.iilfleatherfair.com

Delhi International Leather Fair
www.delhileatherfair.com

Italy
SIMAC (Bologna)
www.simac-fair.assomac.com

Lineapelle (Bologna)
www.lineapelle-fair.it

MICAM (Milan)
www.micamonline.com

Anteprima (Milan)
www.anteprima.lineapelle-fair.it

Mipel (Milan)
www.mipel.com

Kazakhstan
Leshow Kazakhstan (Almaty)
leshow.ru/eng/General–information/
leshow_kazakhstan

Mexico
Anpic (Guadalajara)
www.anpic.com

Middle East
Shoe & Leather Fair Middle East
(Abu Dhabi)
www.leathermiddleeast.com

Syria Leather Fair (Aleppo)
www.webindia.com/syrialeatherfair

Saudi Leather Fair (Riyadh)
www.visionfairs.com/exhibitions/2009/
jeddah/about

Cairo International Leather Fair
www.egyptexport.org/leather/cairo-
international-leather

Russia
LeShow – International Leather & Fur
Fashion Fair (Moscow)
www.leshow.ru/eng

Serbia & Montenegro
International Fair of Textiles, Leather &
Equipment (Belgrade)
www.sajam.co.rs

Singapore
Zak Salaam India
www.zaksalaamindia.com

Spain
Pielespana (Barcelona)
www.pielespana.com

Iberpiel/Modacalzado (Madrid)
www.modacalzado.ifema.es

Sweden
Nordic Shoe & Bag Fair (Stockholm)
www.nordicshoeandbagfair.se

Syria
Damascus Leather Technologies Activities
(DTLA)
www.biztradeshows.com

Thailand
Bangkok International Leather Fair (BIL)
www.thaitradefair.com

Turkey
Istanbul Leather Fashion Fair
www.istanbulderifuari.net/site/eng

Ukraine
Leshow Kiev
www.leshow.ru

United Kingdom
London Fashion Week
www.londonfashionweek.co.uk

Pure London
www.purewomenswear.co.uk

United States
Panamerican Leather Fair (Miami)
www.sifair.com

Vietnam
Saigon Leather & Shoe Fair (SLS)
www.vsp.vn

Shoe & Leather Vietnam (Ho Chi Min City)
www.biztradeshows.com

LEATHER SCHOOLS
Fashion Institute of Technology
Seventh Avenue at 27th Street
New York, NY 10001–5992, USA
www.fitnyc.edu
What the School Offers: Certificate
programme in either men's or women's
leather apparel design.

**Leather Industries of America –
Leather Research Laboratory**
University of Cincinnati
5997 Center Hill Avenue
Cincinnati, OH 45224, USA
www.leatherusa.org
What the School Offers: Research of
industrial and environmental issues, and
monitoring of government regulations. Also
trains technical personnel and provides
technical services and consultations.

**Lederinstitut – German Tanners'
School, Reutlingen**
Postfach 2944, D-72719,
Reutlingen, Germany
www.lgr-reutlingen.de
What the School Offers: Training, research
and experimental institute for leather.

National Institute of Fashion Technology (NIFT)
Hauz Khaus, Near Gulmohar Park
New Delhi, India 110016
www.niftindia.com
What the School Offers: Two-year post graduate diploma in leather garment design and technology.

Texas Tech University – Leather Research Institute
2500 Broadway
Lubbock, TX 79409, USA
www.ttu.edu/campus
What the School Offers: Research, education and services directed at expanding the leather tanning and finished leather products industry in the US.

UNIVERSITY OF NORTHAMPTON
British School of Leather Technology (BSLT)
University of Northampton
Park Campus
Boughton Green Road
Northampton NN2 7AN, UK
www.northampton.ac.uk
What the School Offers: Study in the science of leather technology and tanning.

BLC Leathersellers' Research Centre
www.leathersellers.co.uk

Leather Conservation Centre
www.leatherconservation.org

also in Northampton,
Museum of Leathercraft
Abington Museum, Abington Park, Northampton, UK
www.museumofleathercraft.org

FASHION COLOUR/TREND FORECAST SERVICES

Carlin Group
www.carlin-groupe.com

Color Association
www.colorassociation.com

Color Marketing Group (CMG)
www.colormarketing.org

Color Portfolio
www.colorportfolio.com

The Doneger Group
www.doneger.com

Fashion Information
www.fashioninformation.com

Fashion Snoops
www.fashionsnoops.com

Fashion Windows
www.fashionwindows.com

Henry Doneger Associates Inc.
www.doneger.com

Le Book
www.lebook.com

Pantone, Inc.
www.pantone.com

Peclers Paris
www.peclersparis.com

Promostyl
www.promostyl.com

Snapfashion
www.snapfashion.com

Style.com
www.style.com

Stylesight
www.stylesight.com

Tobe Report
www.tobereport.com

Trendstop
www.trendstop.com

Worth Global Style Network (WGSN)
www.wgsn.com

CLEANING & CARE PRODUCTS

Apple Brand® Products
www.applepolishes.com
Products: Protectorants, leather cleaners & conditioners, suede cleaners

Bick 4®
www.bickmore.com
Products: Leather conditioners, cleaners and protectorants

Footwear Etc.
www.footwearetc.com
Products: Cadillac leather care, Barge cement, Apple shoe care conditioners

The Leather Solution®
www.leathersolutions.com
Product: Leather cleaner, conditioner and protectorants

Lexol®
www.lexol.com
Products: Leather cleaners/conditioners

Orkin of London®
www.orkin.co.uk
Products: Leather/suede protectorants, cleaners and conditioners

Panda International
www.zipppershop.com
Products: Glover's needles, cold tape, awls, cutting blades, cement & thinner, cutting table dressing oil, double-faced tape, granite tag boards, fusible webbing and glazed thread

Scotchgard® by 3M
www.3m.com
Product: Protectorant

GLOSSARY

Abattoir
A slaughterhouse for animals.

Aniline skins
Very soft skins without any sprayed-on additives.

Basifying agents
Chemical agents used to neutralize acidity.

Bating
The process of using vinegar to neutralize lime in an animal's skin.

Bleeding (or staining)
The migration of a dye in a solution from leather into another material, caused by perspiration, laundering or wet weather exposure, largely controlled by the tanner's choice of dye and dyeing conditions.

Blocking
The adhesion of a leather finish to itself.

Bundle
A 12-skin unit.

Chrome
The key element in chromium sulphate, which transforms the natural proteins in skins to inert substances that resist rotting.

Cockles
Bruise marks; veins that appear in irregular patterns on raw skin.

Cold tape
A woven tape with a glove at one side used to control stretch in certain areas of a garment.

Crocking
The physical transfer of colour through a rubbing action.

Crust
A dried, raw animal skin.

Curing
A process that protects animal skins from rotting.

Cuts (or cut lines)
The seams required to make a garment.

Double hiding
A condition where the grain layer is actually separated from the inner corium layer of an animal skin.

English domestic
Lambskin that comes from England.

Fat liquor
A mandatory additive used in the tanning process, it adds oils to animal skins and returns the skins to their natural softness.

Fitting muslin
A first sample of muslin for the purpose of testing the garment for proper fit.

Flaying
Removing skin from an animal carcass, by hand and/or machine.

Fusible interfacing
A support material sold by the yard, which has a gummed adhesive back used to add stiffness to certain areas of a garment.

Grain side
The outside of an animal skin.

Hand
The overall feel of a skin, its stiffness versus its softness.

Hide
The skin of a large animal, such as a cow or horse.

Marking and scissor method
An alternative to the short knife method, in which a waterproof marking pen is used to trace around a pattern piece with a pencil or fine tipped waterproof marking pen to mark all notches; sharp dressmaking shears, usually 17 cm (7 inches) or 25 cm (10 inches) in length, are used to cut pattern pieces.

Mood boards
Theme or concept boards that help the designer sell a particular line to a target customer.

Nappa
The outside (formerly fur-bearing side) of an animal, worn on the outside of a garment.

Neutralization
A wet process used in tanning, where wet blues are processed with specific ingredients designed to make animal skins lighter, softer, harder etc.

Oak-tag pattern
A pattern made of oak-tag paper.

Oil tanning
Leather tanned with animal oils and/or fish oils, producing very soft leather.

Over-splitting
Splitting a thick hide into pieces of leather that are too thin.

Pack
Represents approximately 0.278 sq m (3,000 sq ft) of leather.

Pickling
Treating animal skins with a mixture of water, salt and sulphuric acid for approximately two hours.

Pipey grain
A loose, coarse, puckered appearance on the grain surface of an animal.

Plongé
Cowskin tanned to a soft, subtle hand and feel.

Puering
A process whereby animal skins are treated with natural enzymes found in excrement, employed before the era of modern tanning.

Semi-aniline
Any skin that has undergone a surface treatment, which involves spraying animal skins with coats of dye or plastic film, designed to obscure flaws.

Setting out
The wringing out of animal skins, part of the skin-storing process.

Setting-out machine
A machine with two rollers that wring out extra moisture, part of the skin-storing process.

Shading
Caused by uneven dyeing, this condition exists when different parts of a skin show variations in colour.

Shearling
The skin of a lamb or young sheep. Also known as hair-on leather or suede.

Short knife
A small knife with replaceable blades that is sharpened on a special stone and used to cut animal skins.

Side leather
Usually skins from a horse, cow and buffalo that are cut in half by tanners before being shipped to manufacturers (also called 'half hides').

Skin
The pelt of a small animal.

Spew (or fatty spew)
A leather that develops a white hazy deposit on its surface.

Splits
Thicker cowskin that can be split into two skins.

Staking
Stretching animal skins back to their normal size without rewetting them.

Suede
The inside of an animal skin, worn on the outside of the garment; leather with a napped surface.

Tackiness
A condition where leather feels tacky or sticky and will adhere to almost anything it touches; the condition is usually due to inadequate drying or curing of the finish system.

Tan
To convert (a hide or skin) into leather.

Tannery
A factory that buys raw skins, makes the skins into leather, colours the leather and sells it to garment manufacturers.

Tannin
A substance of plant origin that has a tanning effect, used in tanning and dyeing skins.

Trapunto
A type of quilting that outlines a design motif using a single stitch and padding in between two layers, resulting in a raised or 'puffy' effect.

Tricot fusible interfacing
A gummed adhesive knit fabric used as a support material.

Weight
The number of grams per square metre (ounces per square foot) of skin.

Wet blues
Defleshed, pickled animal skins that have had chromium sulphate powder, among other ingredients, added to them, and have been rotated in drums for roughly eight hours; skins turn a light blue colour when they emerge from the drums.

White handkerchief test
A test used to confirm the stability of a garment's colour by rubbing a handkerchief along the inner facing of the garment; the colour should not come off easily.

FURTHER READING

BIBLIOGRAPHY

Churchill, James. *The Complete Book of Tanning Skins and Furs*. Stackpole Books, Harrisburg, PA, 1983.

Delano, Joseph. *The New Book of Leatherwork: Projects for Today*. Drake Publishers, New York, NY, 1974.

DiValentin, Maria M. *Getting Started in Leathercraft*. Collier Books, New York, NY, 1972.

Furst, Ronald Kenneth. *Soft Suede, Supple Leather*. Simon and Schuster, New York, NY, 1974.

Gustavson, K. H. *The Chemistry of Tanning Processes*. Academic Press, New York, NY, 1956.

Hamilton-Head, Ian. *Leatherwork*. Blandford Press, Poole, Dorset, England, 1979.

Kanigel, Robert. *Faux Real*. Joseph Henry Press, Washington, D.C., 2007.

Leather Industries of America proprietary publications
(available from www.leatherusa.com/LIA-Publications.htm):
Dictionary of Leather Terminology. Tanners' Council of America, New York, NY, 1969.
Leather Facts (John W. Mitchell) New England Tanners' Club, Peabody, MA, 1983.
Trade Practices for Proper Packer Cattlehide Delivery (with United States Hide, Skin & Leather Association). Arlington, VA, 1985.

Loeb, Jo. *The Leather Book: Leather Clothes & Furniture You Can Make Yourself*. Prentice-Hall, Inc., Englewood Cliffs, NJ, 1975.

Manning, Mary and E. A. *Leatherwork, A Step-by-Step Guide*. Hamlyn Publishing Group, London, 1974.

John Minnoch and Sterling Robert Minnoch (eds). *Hides and Skins*. National Hide Association, Sioux City, IA, 1979.

Morris, Ben and Elizabeth. *Making Clothes in Leather*. Taplinger Publishing Company, Englewood Cliffs, NJ, 1975.

O'Flaherty, Fred, and Roddy, William T. (eds). *The Chemistry and Technology of Leather* (4 vols). Kreiger Publishing Co., Malabar, FL, 1956–65; repr. 1978.

Parker, Xenia Ley. *Working with Leather*. Charles Scribner's Sons, New York, NY, 1972.

Quilleriet, Anne-Laure. *The Leather Book*. Assouline Publishing, New York, NY, 2004.

Sharphouse, J. H. *Leather Technician's Handbook*. Leather Producer's Association, Moulton Park, Northampton, England, 1983.

Thorstensen, Thomas C., *Practical Leather Technology*, 2d rev. ed., R. E. Krieger, Huntington, NY, 1969; repr. 1976.

Waterer, John W. *Leather Craftsmanship*. Frederick A. Praeger, New York, 1968; and *Leather in Life, Art and Industry*. Faber & Faber, London, 1946.

Welsh, Peter C., *Tanning in the United States to 1850*. Smithsonian Institution, Washington, D. C., 1964.

PERIODICALS AND PUBLICATIONS

Italy
Arpel
Colori in Pelle
Vogue Pelle

France
Le Cuir
IDC Industrie Du Cuir

Leather International Magazine
www.leathermag.com

International Leather Guide
www.leatherbuyersguide.info

Women's Wear Daily
www.wwd.com

WEBSITES

Biztradeshows
www.biztradeshows.com

BLC Leather Technology Centre online resource
www.all-about-leather.co.uk

Bvents
www.bvents.com

Infomat
www.infomat.com

International Trade Center online resource
www.intracen.org/leatherline/leather_guide.htm

Leather Pages
www.leatherpages.com

Vegetarian Resource Group
www.vrg.org

INDEX

Page numbers in **bold** refer to picture captions.

abattoirs 60, 61, 186
Adolfo **23**
Alaïa, Azzedine 12, 24, **26**, 30, **31**
Alcantara® 171
alligator **75**, 86
Amaretta® 172
anaconda 85
Andrew Marc 76, 78, **79**
animal rights issues 12, 172
antelope 67, 84
Armani, Giorgio 24, **25**, 28
armholes **26**, **42**, 112, 124, 125, 155, 177
Aztecs 16

Baby Phat **170**
Balenciaga **60**
Bally 40, **41**, 56, **57**
belts/belt loops **21**, **42**, **43**, 52, 132, 136
Beretta, Anne Marie **24**
Betten, Jordan (Lost Art) **7**, 46, **47**, **54**, 76, **77**, **93**, **120**
black leather 12, 19, **21**, 22, **24**, **31**
bondage look 12, **52**
boots 15, 16, **43**, **50**, 86
Bottega Veneta **48**
Brando, Marlon 12, 19
Braniff Airlines 170, **171**
buckskin 16, 84
buffalo 16, 60
bustiers **12**, **35**, **74**, **108**

cabretta 84
Calamity Jane **17**
calfskin **20**, **56**, 84
capeskin 84
care of leather 13, 84, 88, 109, 162, 164–5, 182, 185
    faux leather/suede **170**, 178, 179
Cashin, Bonnie 19, 20, **31**, **92**
Cavalli, Enrico **74**
Cavalli, Roberto **44**
Celine **36**
Chai, Richard 54, **55**
chamois 84
Chanel 12, 50
chaps 12, 16, **21**
China 12, 15
Christensen, Helena **33**
chrome/chromium sulphate 13, 64, 65, 186
Clarino® 172
Coach **19**
coats 12
    design/spec sheets 94–9
    trench coats 18, **36**, **41**, **48**, **49**, 170, **171**
    twentieth-century design 18, **20**, **24**, **26**, **28**, **29**, **33**, **36**, **37**, **140**, **171**
    twenty-first century design **38**, **39**, **40**, **41**, 44, **45**, **48**, **82**, **83**, 170
cobra 85
cold tape 113, 117, 121, 122, 130, 134–5, 142–4, 186
collars **37**, 112, 113, 116, 122, 123–4, 144, 153, 154
colour
    in history 14, 15, **17**

matching 87, 103, 104, 105
    problems *see under* quality control issues
    twentieth-century design 19, **23**, **27**, **31**, **34**, **104**
    twenty-first century design 38, **44**, 48, **49**, **56**
    see also black leather
corsets 12, **17**, **27**
cowboys 12, 16
cowskin 24, 82, 84, 187
crocodile 60, 61, 86
Crow, Sheryl **47**
cutting 103
    cut lines 82, 88, 89
    cutting boards 104
    faux leather 174
    marking and scissor method 104, **105**, 174, 186
    from patterns 104, 105
    planning 82, 87, 88–9, 105, 174
    procedure 104
    short knife method 104, 187
    suede 105
    tips 105

D-Squared **48**
darts **50**, 130, 174, 178
de la Renta, Oscar **27**
Dean, James 19
decorative techniques **44**, 71
    beads 14, 16, **17**, 20
    braiding **15**, 20, **75**
    burnishing 13, **33**, 38, **39**
    embossing 24, 38, 50, 86, 105
    embroidery 13, **16**, **20**, **23**, 71
    fringing 12, 16, **17**, 20
    glazing 38, 68
    in history 14, 15, 16, **17**
    laser cutting 13, 38, **39**, 40, 71
    metallicizing 13, **32**, 38, **39**, 71, **74**, 76
    modern techniques 13, 20, 24
    ombré effects 13, **34**
    painting 15, 16, 20, 24, **45**
    pearlizing 86
    printing **20**, 24, 28, **46**, 66, 71, 76, 86, 105
    weaving **54**, 71
deerskin 12, 16, **17**, 60, 84
Demeulemeester, Ann **34**, **38**
design process **75**
    the customer 74, 76
    design/spec sheets 91, 92, 94–101
    inspiration 74, **75**, 76, **77**
    merchandising 78
    organizing the collection 76, 78
    research 74
    samples 76, 78, 92
    sketches **75**, 78
di Sant'Angelo, Giorgio **23**
Dior 12, 50, **140**
distressing 38, 40, **41**, **60**, 71, 86
doeskin 84
Dolce & Gabbana **38**, **46**, 50, **51**, 172
doublets **15**
dresses
    in history 14, **16**
    suede **23**, **162**
    twentieth-century design **23**, **28**, **33**, **34**, **171**, 172, **173**, **175**

twenty-first century design **38**, **39**, 40, **75**, **162**, **172**
dry-cleaning 88, 109, 164–5, **170**, 179, 182
Duckie Brown **56**
DuPont **13**, 74, 112, 170

Easy Rider 19
eelskin **46**
Egyptians 14–15
elephant 85
elk 60, 84
Etruscans 15

fabric combinations **30**, 40, **41**, **52**
fabric-to-leather translations 83
fastenings
    buttons/buttonholes **42**, 76, **79**, 112, 123, 135, 144–5, 147, 159
    frogs **116**
    lacing 14, **15**, 20, **31**, **42**
    safety pins **33**
    turn-key closures **19**
    zips **19**, **29**, 48, **60**, 112, 113, 133, 134
faux leather 169, **175**
    care **170**, 178, 179
    construction techniques 174–9
    cutting 174
    faux grain leather 172, 174, 178, 179
    faux suede 170–1, 172, 174, 178, 179
    in history 170–1, 172
    needle sizes 174
    patent leather 172, **173**, 174, 178, 179
    pressing 179
    seams 174, 176–7
    stitch length 174
    stitching 174, 178
Fendi 32, **33**, **34**
Ferragamo **42**
Ferre, Gianfranco **32**
fetishism 12, 28, **29**
film influences 12, 19, 74
fish skins **46**, 60, 86
fitting muslins 88, 186
footwear 14, 15, 16, 166 *see also* boots
forecast services 74, 185
France 16, 28
frog 86

Galliano, John **42**, **50**
Gaultier, Jean Paul 12, **40**
gauntlets 16, **32**
Gernreich, Rudi **20**
Givenchy 42, **43**
gloves 16, **44**, **140** *see also* gauntlets
gluing 109, 116, 122, 124, 130, 135, 153, 154, 174
goat suede 84
goatskin 15, **24**, 60, 67, 82, 85, 166
Greeks 12
Gucci 12, **28**, 34

hair sheep 85
Halston 170, **171**
hand-lacing 36, **47**, **108**, 167
hand-sewing 14, **47**, 108, 109, **120**, 125, 137
hats 16, **18**
Hebrews 15
Hell's Angels 12, 19

hems **26**, **39**, **40**, **49**, 109, 164, 178, 182
Hermès 46, 48, **49**, 54, **112**
Herrera, Alicia 24
hides
    defined 82, 186
    in history 7, 12, 14
    see also skins
hip-hop **27**, 74
hippie fashion 12, 20, 22, **23**
hippopotamus 85
history of leather 12, 14–17, 170–1, 172
Hoban, Michael **27**
horse 19, 60, 85
House of Field 171

Incas 16
insulation 112
interfacing 112, 121, 122, 129, 130, 142–4, 156–7
    fusible interfacing 112, **113**, 176, 186
    tricot interfacing 112, 187
interlinings 112
Italy 12, 15, 28, **42**, 68

jackets
    aviator 12, 19, **30**
    bomber 12, 40, 140–59
    construction techniques 112, 140–59
    design/spec sheets 94–9
    '8-ball' **27**
    in history 16, **17**
    motorcycle 12, 19
    sleeveless **55**, **57**
    suede 12, **31**, **32**
    twentieth-century design **18**, 19, **24**, **27**, **29**,
    30, **31**, **32**, **35**, **36**, **92**, **116**, 172, **173**
    twenty-first century design **42**, **46**, 48, **50**, **53**,
    54, **55**, **56**, **57**, **60**, **75**, **112**
Jacobs, Marc **53**
Jagger, Mick 12
jerkins **15**
Jitrois, Jean Claude **13**, **54**, **83**
jodhpurs **55**
jumpsuits **42**, 48, **49**, 74

Kane, Christopher **52**
kangaroo 60
Karan, Donna 12
kidskin 84, 85
Klein, Anne **22**
Klein, Calvin 12, **27**
Kors, Michael 24, **44**
Kravitz, Lenny **93**
Kuraray Co., Ltd 172

Lacroix, Christian **30**
Lagerfeld, Karl **33**, **50**
lamb suede **24**, 84, 88, 112
lambskin 12
    characteristics 60
    coats **36**, **83**
    English domestic 60, 85, 186
    manufacturing process 62
    size 85
    tanning process 64, 67
    trousers **54**, **83**
    weight 85
    see also shearling
Landau, Adrienne 24

Lars, Byron **30**
Lauren, Ralph 12, **116**
Leather Industries Research Laboratory 162, 164
Leatherette 170
linings 112, 123, 125, 135–6, 157–9, 165, 178
lizard 61, 85
Lost Art **167**, **182** *see also* Betten, Jordan
Lupino, Ida **18**

3M 112
Madonna 12
Malandrino **82**
Marni 36, **37**
The Matrix 12
MaxMara **52**
Mayans 16
McCartney, Stella 13
McDonald, Julien 42
McQueen, Alexander 38, **39**, 42, **43**, **46**
military influences 40, **41**, 44, **45**, 50, **51**
Miu Miu 52, **53**, 172
Mizrahi, Isaac 30
Montana, Claude 12, **24**, **32**
mood boards *see* theme boards
Moors 15
Morrison, Jim 12
Mugler, Thierry 12, 28, **29**, 34, **108**

Native Americans 12, 16, **17**
    influence on design **23**, **42**, 44, **45**
Naugahyde 170
Nelson, Willie **120**
Nevelson, Louise **75**
North Beach Leather 24, **27**
novelty skins **46**, 71, 86
nubuck 86, 182

'One Star' Perfecto motorcycle jacket **19**
ostrich 50, **51**, 85
Owens, Rick 48, **49**, 56

patchwork **23**, 71, **82**, **104**
patent leather **46**, 71, 86, 172, **173**, 174, 178, 179
patterns
    and cutting 104, 105
    design/spec sheets 92
    jacket 141
    lining patterns 112
    oak-tag patterns 89, 186
    pattern cutters 89
    planning stage 88–9, 174, 178
    shirt 121
    templates 89, 133, 147
    trousers 129
peccary 60, 85
Perfecto motorcycle jacket 19
Pertegaz, Manuel 20, **21**
PETA (People for the Ethical Treatment of Animals)
    12, 172
Phoenicians 15
pig suede 84, 88, 105
pigskin 13, 24, 60, 84, 85
planning the design 82, 83, 88–9, 174, 178
pleather 170
pleats **53**, 130, 152
plongé **13**, 187
pockets **48**, 112, 113, 116, 122, 130–2, 144,
    146–52

ponchos **16**
pony 85
Posen, Zac 44, **45**
prehistoric peoples 14
Presley, Elvis 12
pressing 109, 176, 178, 179, 182
processing skins
    bating 62, 186
    chemical treatments 62
    curing 61–2, 186
    defleshing 62, **63**
    dehairing 62
    drying 61, 62, **63**, 65, 66, **67**, 70
    flaying 61, 186
    killing the animal 61
    pickling 62, 186
    polishing 68
    refrigeration 61
    salting 13, 62, 186
    setting out 65, 187
    see also tanning process
protective clothing 12, 15, 16, **19**, **27**
punk fashion 12, 19
PVC 170
python 60, 86

quality control issues 162
    abrasion resistance 88, 164
    blocking 164, 186
    colour problems
        bleeding/staining 88, 163, 171, 186, 187
        crocking 162, 171, 186
        fading 162
    corrosion resistance 164
    double hiding 166, 186
    finish adhesion 164
    mould/mildew 165, 182
    odour 166
    oil spotting 165
    pipey grain 166, 187
    shrinkage 164–5, **170**
    spew 165
    strength problems 163–4
    tackiness 164, 187
    testing 88, 162, **163**, 164, 187
    variations in appearance 166
    water spotting 70, 165

rabbit **46**
Rebel Without a Cause 19
religion and leather 12
Ricci, Nina **20**
rock music influences 12, 19, 46, **47**, 74, 76
Romans 15
Rucci, Ralph **75**
Rutland, Frank H. 9, 162

safari suits **21**
Saint Laurent, Yves 20, **21**
salmon 60, 86
Sander, Jil 28, **29**
Sarasola, Lisandro 24
schools 184–5
Schott Bros. 19
Schultz, Augustus 16
seal 86
seams 115
    clipping 116, 124, 135, 153

decorative **31**, **42**
double/triple needle 117
faux leather 174, 176–7
mock flat fell 117
open and glued 109, 116, 122, 124, 130, 135, 153, 154
raw edge lapped and stitched 117
reinforcing 113
rolling 109, 116, 122, 124
seam allowances 89, 116, 122, 124, 130, 174
sewing machines 108, 178
sex and leather 12, 32, 42, **44** *see also* fetishism
shark 60, 85
shearling 187
size and weight 85
in twentieth-century designs **25**, **32**, **34**, 36, **140**
in twenty-first century designs 38, **39**, **40**, **42**, 44, **45**, 48, **49**, **50**, **55**
sheepskin 84, 85, 166
'shell cordovan' 85
shirts **17,** 52, **120**
construction techniques 120–5
design/spec sheets 94–9
suede **18**, **140**
shorts **92**
shrinking 67, 105, 164–5, **170**, 182
skins
aniline skins 66, 69, 70, 87, 186
appropriateness 88
blemishes **39**, 61, 65, 66, 70, 83, 85, 87, 166
see also quality control issues
bundles 87, 186
characteristics 84–6
cockles 61, 65, 186
colour matching 87, 103, 104, 105
crusts 62, **63**, 64, 65, 186
cutting *see* cutting
decoration *see* decorative techniques
defined 82, 187
dyeing *see under* tanning process
grading 66, 69
grain 60, 66, 87, **104**, 105, 166, 186, 187
hand 82, **170**, 171, 186
measuring 69, 82, 83
names of parts 87
nappa 50, 66, **67,** 68, 87, 186
packs 87, 186
processing *see* processing skins
purchasing 60–1, 87
quality 60, 64, 69, 70, 87
selecting 60, 82, 88, 103
semi-aniline skins 66, 69, 70, 87, 187
shading 85, 87, 166, 187
side leather 82, 187
size 82–3, 84, 85, 87
sorting 65–6, **69**, 103, 104
splits 13, 60, 84, 163–4
spray treatments 70, 87
storing 65, 104, 105
strength 84, 163, 164
tanning *see* tanning process
thickness 82, 88, 163, 164
weight 82, 84, 85, 86, 187
see also suede; types of skin
skirts 12
design/spec sheets 100–1

in history **16**
suede **18**
twentieth-century design **18**, **22**, **24**, **27**, **108**, **140**
twenty-first century design **46**, **50**, 52, **53**, **57**
sleeves **15**, **27**, **35**, 122, 124, 146, 154–5
snakeskin **30**, **43**, 60, 85, 86, **93**
Solofra, Italy 15
Spain 15, **21**
speciality skins **46**, 60, 61, **75**, 86
splits/splitting 13, 16, 187
sports clothing 18
stamping 13, 15, **35**, 42
Sterlacci, Francesca 24
stitching
basting 174
decorative **26**, **43**, **44**, **49**
equipment 108, 178
faux leather 174, 178
handstitching **47**
topstitching **49**, 108
see also seams
storing
garments 179, 182
skins 65, 104, 105
The Story of O 12
stretch leather 12, 13, **54**, 71, **83**
strips, leather **54**, **167**
style boards 76, 78
styling tape 88
suede 18, 24, 36
appropriateness 88
care 182
colour problems 162
cutting 105, 174
faux suede 170–1, 172, 174, 178, 179
manufacturing process 64, 66, **67**, 68
Sui, Anna 171, **172**
suits
twentieth-century design **20**, **21**, **26**, **35**, **172**
twenty-first century design 40, **41**, 48, **49**, **75**
see also jumpsuits; trouser suits
Sumerians 14
symbolism 12, 22

tanning process 12, 187
basifying agents 64, 186
chemical tanning 13, 16, 64, 65, 166
dyeing 14, 15, **23**, 66, **67**, 70, 87, 162, 163
see also colour
fat/fat liquor 14, 15, 60, 64, 66, 165, 186
finishing 68, 164
in history 14, 15
neutralization 65, 66, 186
oil tanning 14, 16, 84, 165, 166, 186
puering 166, 187
purpose 60
re-tanning **64**, 65
staking 67, 187
vegetable tanning 13, 14, 65
wet blues **64**, 65, 187
see also processing skins
theme boards 76, 78, **79**, 186
Thimister, Josephus 38, **39**, **162**
Toi, Zang **104**
tops **27**, **54**
topstitching 116, 117, 125, 131, 133–4, 137, 150, 151, 177

Toray Industries 170, 171
trade organizations/trade press 74, 183
trade shows 74, 183–4
trapunto 46, 187
tree bark 13, 14, 15, 65
trenchsuits 48, **49**
trouser suits 40, **41**, 128
trousers 12, **182**
construction techniques 128–37
design/spec sheets 100–1
in history 15, **17**
suede **32**
twentieth-century design **19**, **29**, **31**, **32**, **128**
twenty-first century design **43**, **44**, **47**, **48**, **54**, **55**, **57**, **83**
see also chaps; trouser suits
tunics 52
twentieth-century design 13
1900–1950s 18–19
1960s–1970s 20–3, **92**, 170, **171**
1980s 24–9, 172, **173**
1990s 30–7, **104**, **108**, 172, **173**, **175**
twenty-first century design 12–13, 38
2000–2004 38–47, **60**, **82**, **162**, **172**
2005–2009 48–57, **75**, **83**, **112**, **170**

Ultraleather® 172
Ultrasuede® 170–1, 172
Ungaro, Emanuel 24, **26**, **36**, 172, **173**
uniform 12, **17**, 18, 170, **171**

Valentino 24, **25**, 40, **41**
vealskin 60, 85
Versace, Gianni 12, 28, 32, **33**, 172, **173**, **175**
Vuitton 52, **53**

waistbands 112, 113, 130, 135, 136–7, 144, 152
waistcoats 16
warm-up suits **75**
washing 13, 84, 165, **170**, 171, 178, 179
Westwood, Vivienne 24, **27**, **128**
whip snake 86
The Wild One 12, 19
Williamson, Matthew 44, **45**
wool **36**, 40, **41**, 62

CREDITS AND ACKNOWLEDGEMENTS

Picture credits

The author and publisher would like to thank the following for providing images for use in this book. In all cases, every effort has been made to credit the copyright holders, but should there be any omissions or errors the publisher would be pleased to insert the appropriate acknowledgement in any subsequent edition of this book.

L=left, R=right, T=top, B=bottom, M=middle:

p2–3: Painted Pants – Courtesy of Lost Art Studio, photo by Tom Kletecka

p4: Jean Claude Jitrois – PARIS: Look Book Images 2008/9

p6: Betten Desk – Courtesy of Lost Art Studio, photo by Tom Kletecka

p13: Jean Claude Jitrois – PARIS: Look Book Images 2008/9

p14: Photo: akg-images/Erich Lessing

p15L: From the Museum of Leathercraft collection

p15R: © V&A Images, Victoria and Albert Museum

p16T/16B/17TL: Heard Museum, Phoenix, Arizona

p17TR: Hulton Archive/Getty Images

p17B: © V&A Images, Victoria and Albert Museum

p18L: Hulton Archive/Getty Images: photograph by Sasha

p18R: Hulton Archive/Getty Images: photograph by Margaret Chute

p19T: Photograph courtesy of Schott Bros.

p19M: © 2001-2009 by Corbis Corporation

p19B: Bonnie Cashin. Tunic and skirt, 1968. Leather and brass. Gift of Mr. Phillip Sills. 1980. c.100.A-B Jacket, late 1950s. Leather and brass. Gift of Genevieve Roach. 2002.58.A-B and coat, late 1950s. Leather. Gift of Mrs. James S. Tomes. 2000.98. Photo by Ken Howie

p23R: Giorgio di Sant' Angelo. Dress, late 1970s. Nylon and Lycra. Gift of Mrs. Patrick Mather. 2002.129. Photo by Ken Howie

p27R: Courtesy of The Museum at FIT

p47: Sheryl Crow – Courtesy of Lost Art Studio, photo by Tara Canova

p54L: Fringed Top – Courtesy of Lost Art Studio, photo by Rennio Maifredi

p54R: Jean Claude Jitrois – PARIS: Look Book Images 2008/9

p56: Courtesy of Duckie Brown

p63–71: Photographs courtesy of Peter Cools, Sales Manager of Motta Alfredo Tannery, Milan, Italy

p75: Courtesy of Ralph Rucci

p77T–B: Betten at Work Table, photo by Annie Schlechter/Wall of Photos, photo by Neil Hilkemeyer/ Inspiration Table, photo by Tom Kletecka – all Courtesy of Lost Art Studio

p79: Courtesy of Andrew Marc

p83R: Jean Claude Jitrois – PARIS: Look Book Images 2008/9

p93: Lenny Kravitz – Courtesy of Lost Art Studio, photo by Mark Seliger

p104T: Photograph by Francesca Sterlacci

p108TL: Photography courtesy of Juki Corporation, Juki America, Inc.

p108BL: Image of Brother Nouvelle PQ 1500S from Brother Industries, Ltd.

p118: Willie Nelson – Courtesy of Lost Art Studio, photo by Mark Seliger

p167: Leather Laces – Courtesy of Lost Art Studio, photo by Tom Kletecka

p168: Courtesy of Baby Phat by Kimora Lee Simmons

p170: Courtesy of Ultrasuede® (America), Inc.

p171T: Courtesy of The Museum at FIT

p171B: Courtesy Dallas Historical Society. Used by permission.

p172L: Image courtesy of Anna Sui, photographer: Raoul Gatchalian

p180–1: Wall of Pants – Courtesy of Lost Art Studio, photo by Annie Schlechter

Additional credits:

The following images are supplied, with special thanks, by © The Fashion Group Foundation, Inc.: p10, 20–22, 23L, 24–26, 27L, 28–46,48–53, 55, 57–58, 72, 80, 90, 102, 106, 110, 114, 126, 140, 160, 172R, 173, 175.

Illustrations for Chapters 10, 11 and 12 by Dobriana Gheneva.

Illustrations for Chapters 4, 9, 14 drawn by, and all illustrations coloured by, Advanced Illustrations Limited.

Author's acknowledgements

Many people helped in the preparation of this book but the one person who helped most of all was my wonderful husband, Jeff Purvin. His understanding, patience, support, guidance and love made this book possible. I would also like to thank my son Colton, who continues to inspire me to be a good role model and who will always be the centre of my universe.

I am eternally indebted to my mother and father, Norma and Frank, and siblings, Arleen, Fay and Paul, who have encouraged my passion for fashion since childhood. I dedicate this book to my entire family.

I would also like to thank the following people:

- Laurence King, Lee Ripley, Anne Townley and Zoe Antoniou for their vision in making this book not just a revision. Their collective energy inspired a newer, more exciting version that is much more creative, current and informative.
- Dobriana Gheneva for her wonderful illustrations in chapters 10, 11 and 12 and for making her former professor even more proud of her, if that is possible.
- Jeannette Nostra, President of GIII Apparel Group for writing the foreword with Carl Katz, contributing design/spec sheets and a jacket as a sewing example, and, most of all, for our lasting friendship.
- Morris Goldfarb, CEO of GIII Apparel Group, my guardian angel, who helped and supported my effort in bringing FIT's leather programme to fruition.
- Chris Gbur, Jose Madera and Barbara Hendieh at GIII Apparel Group for too many contributions to enumerate.
- Peter Cools for his tannery images and never-ending patience, and Alfredo Motta at Motta Alfredo tannery in Milan.
- Mitch Alfus of Libra Leather for his friendship and expertise about the leather industry, tanneries and the most current techniques in the industry.
- Frank H. Rutland, former Technical Director of the Leather Industries Research Laboratory at the University of Cincinnati, for his significant assistance in the chapter on leather defects.
- Jordan Betten and Ralph Rucci for the use of photos of their work and design studios. And their staff – Neil Hilkemeyer (Lost Art); Rosina Rucci, Coco Mitchell and Angharad Coates (Chado Ralph Rucci).
- Patty Munro, Keiji Obata and Robert Stier of Toray Ultrasuede (America), Inc. for their help researching and collecting images of faux suede.
- Margaret Hayes, Edith Loss and Jean Meeks-Barker at the Fashion Group International for the use of the Fashion Group Archive.
- Dennita Sewell and Ken Howie at the Phoenix Art Museum; Diana Pardue at the Heard Museum; Irving Solero and Fred Dennis at the museum at FIT.
- David Valdez (Juki Sewing Machine Company) and June Mellinger (Brother Sewing Machine Company).
- Korea Merchandise Testing & Research Institute for providing me with a leather test report.
- Leather factories Marcella Leather and Monkey Head for allowing me to photograph the original step-by-step construction for the shirt, trousers and jacket.